St Mary's Church as it might have looked in Saxon times

TWO MILLENNIA OF VILLAGE LIFE

A HISTORY OF EAST LEAKE

OWEN WOOD

WRITTEN TO COMMEMORATE THE CENTENARY OF THE PARISH COUNCIL, 1895 - 1995
AND IN CELEBRATION OF THE YEAR 2000

St Mary's Church as it is today

TWO MILLENNIA OF VILLAGE LIFE
A HISTORY OF EAST LEAKE

First published in Great Britain 1999
by East Leake Parish Council
45 Main Street, East Leake, Loughborough,
Leicestershire, LE12 6PF

Copyright of text © 1999 by R Owen Wood
Copyright of design © 1999 by Keith Wood

A CIP catalogue record for this title is available
from the British Library
ISBN 0 9535103 0 1

Printed and bound in Great Britain by Abbey Print
Services Ltd, Nottingham

This book is sold subject to the condition that it
shall not by way of trade or otherwise, be lent,
resold, hired out, or otherwise circulated without
the publisher's prior consent in any form of binding
or cover other than that in which it is published
and without a similar condition including this
condition being imposed on the subsequent
purchaser

CONTENTS

Acknowledgements	*1*
The Author	*2*
Foreword	*3*
Introduction	*4*
Part One — Early Times	1
Iron Age Farming and the Roman Occupation	1
The Early Saxon Period AD 410 - 900	3
Part Two — A Medieval Agricultural Community	4
A Picture of the Medieval Parish	6
The Leake Family and the Chief Manor	7
Family Tree of the Leakes of Leake and Sutton Scarsdale	9
Family Tree of Stauntons, Shirleys and Ferrers	11
Part Three — Thirteenth to Eighteenth Centuries	13
The Town of Leake — a Medieval Community	13
The Treaty of Leake	13
Local Administration	14
The Homesteads and the Yeomen	14
The Town Lands Trust	15
John Bley circa 1674 - 1731	18
Tradesmen, Craftsmen and Other Occupations	20
The Church of Leke — the Ecclesiastical Body	21
St Leonard's and St Mary's Church at Great Leake	21
Non-conformity	24
Part Four — Farming and Enclosure	26
Enclosure	26
Farming — Nineteenth and Twentieth Centuries	29
Part Five — Industries of East Leake	40
Weaving	40
Framework Knitting — Lace and Hosiery	40
Stocking Frame and the Hosiery Industry	41
Basket Making	43
Gypsum and Plaster	45
Part Six — Modern Times	48
Education	48
The Care of the Poor	49
Great Central Railway	49
Local Government — The Parish Council	50
The Last Fifty Years 1948 - 1998	51

Part seven — The Parish Council	54
Appendix 1 — Chairmen and Clerks	62
Appendix 2 — Council Membership at Various Times	63
Appendix 3 — Examples of Finance at Various Stages in the Council's History	65
Bibliography	67
1884 Map of the Village	70
1999 Map of the Village	71

TERMINOLOGY AND SPELLING

Readers are reminded that certain names and terms for titles, occupations, payments and dues have been in common use since the eleventh century. However, today's understanding of many of these differs from earlier definitions.

Similarly, until recently spelling has not been standardised. In particular, names of places and people have varied even over short periods and within the same document. The spelling commonly adopted in any period is the spelling used in the text of this book applying to that period. The actual spelling used in a specific document is also used when referring to it in the text.

ACKNOWLEDGEMENTS

Many people during my lifetime have contributed to my knowledge of the history of East Leake. It is impossible to name them all individually.

In the last twenty years, members of the Local History Group have contributed in many ways to the research into the history of the village and likewise identifying individual contributions is also virtually impossible.

My thanks are due to Tony Grundy for his help, especially in producing maps, diagrams, etc.

The production of the work owes much to the collaboration of those directly involved.

I am not able in the use of of a computer or typewriter. Madeline Lord had volunteered to undertake work for the Parish Council and she has helped in preparing the script from my handwritten notes — not the best of writing. Mollie Jacques and Keith Hodgkinson were delegated by the Parish Council to "oversee" the work. They did much more.

The research by Mollie Jacques into the minutes of the Parish Council resulted in a summary which I decided to incorporate in its entirety into the book.

Keith Hodgkinson was the first vice chairman of the local history group and his professional contribution far exceeded the brief from the Parish Council. I am very grateful to him for checking some aspects of history on which I was not so well informed, for his contribution to proof reading and to the general structure of the book.

Photographs and illustrations have been obtained from a number of sources — A History of East Leake by the Rev Sidney Pell Potter, the Nottinghamshire County Archives, British Gypsum Limited, David Clarke, Jim Cockayne, Charlie and P R Firth and Keith Wood. Their interest in the copyright of these photographs and illustrations is hereby acknowledged.

Finally I owe a great deal to my son, Keith. At the outset he volunteered to help me. He is in business as a public relations consultant and has carried through the many aspects of preparing the book for the printer and the many tasks involved in publishing.

Owen Wood

Images used in the design of the front and back covers and elsewhere herein were obtained from IMSI's MasterClips/MasterPhotos© Collection, 1895 Francisco Blvd East, San Rafael, CA 94901-5506, USA.

THE AUTHOR

The author has lived in East Leake for sixty years. He was an agricultural economist at Sutton Bonington, an agricultural college and later a department of the University of Nottingham, School of Agriculture. As such he was concerned with the relationship between the decisions of farmers and the need to meet changes in farming. This required a knowledge of the history of farming and the impact of changes upon related policy decisions.

At an early age he became interested in social and local history. By the late 1940s he was involved in the history of both East and West Leake. For a number of years he attended joint University/WEA classes.

In 1978 he tutored a six week course on the history of East Leake at the end of which a local history group was formed, and he became the chairman.

THE PARISH COUNCIL

East Leake Parish Council is proud to present this account of a village. While describing the changes in human activity and achievement as played out in a local setting, it also demonstrates the continuity which underpins the history of Britain as a whole and we hope it finds favour as representing more than just the story of a few square miles.

The Parish Council has only existed for a small proportion of the period covered by the book, but has itself changed much in its first century. Where we all go from here will provide material for future historians. We hope they will have as many interesting events and people to get to understand as the present researchers have enjoyed.

But without the support of British Gypsum, who under-wrote all the printing costs, the fruits of their labours would not have seen the light of day. The Parish Council, on behalf of the village, acknowledges this generosity.

Mollie Jacques
Chairman, East Leake Parish Council
February 1999

FOREWORD

I have great pleasure in writing a few words as a Foreword to this tremendous book on East Leake.

Those of you who read this book will learn of the village's fascinating history but in one industry, plasterboard production, the name 'East Leake' is already known around the world. Gypsum-based activity started here over a hundred years ago and plasterboard has been manufactured here for over fifty years. During this time, British Gypsum at East Leake has been a leading centre of research, product development, and manufacturing and the flagship has hosted visitors from every corner of the world. East Leake has genuinely been at the leading edge of a global industry.

British Gypsum's relationship with the village has been a happy one with many of the company's employees having lived here for generations. Our high level of investment in the region has been justified by the commitment and skill level of the local people who have worked for the company during that time.

Paul Withers
Managing Director
British Gypsum
(A subsidiary of BPB PLC)
February 1999

INTRODUCTION

This history builds on two earlier publications on the history of East Leake — "The Antiquities of Nottinghamshire" by Dr Robert Thoroton, 1677, and "A History of East Leake" by Rev Sidney Pell Potter, 1903. Since then there have been booklets and publications by sundry authors and by the East Leake and District Local History Group.

In 1995 the centenary of the formation of the Parish Council called for an updated history to include the events of the twentieth century and the advances in our knowledge of English history since the nineteenth century.

The history is complicated. Administratively East Leake and West Leake have always been separate civil communities. East Leake was in Rushcliffe Wapentake and West Leake in Plumtree Wapentake. However, the Rectory was, from the tenth century up until 1882, a single benefice. In this publication both civil and ecclesiastical matters applying solely to West Leake have been excluded.

In addition, as this history marks a hundred years of the Parish Council, it describes the council's contribution to the history of East Leake and traces the civil administration since the tenth century through the medieval courts of the hundreds, and the parish vestries composed of the chief lords, the manor lords and the freemen — the English democratic system.

The name "Leake" is derived from the Old English word "Lecche" meaning a water meadow, and indicates a Saxon settlement between 410 and 600 AD. At the time of Domesday, 1086, it was the area approximately that of the parishes of East and West Leake. There have been several variations in the name, both of the village and of the family which settled here in the eleventh century — Lecche, Leche, Lake, Leke, Great Leake, Ester Leke, Town of Leke and East Leake. Throughout the medieval period from the tenth and eleventh centuries to the eighteenth and nineteenth centuries, legal documents generally refer to it as the Town of Leake otherwise Great Leake.

A township is an ancient and stable unit of local administration — older than and outliving the manor. The Town of Leake or Great Leake was a community of the families of lords of the manors, freemen, villeins and bordars, perhaps better identified as gentry, landowners, farmers, and their workers and servants. It is their story that this book describes.

Today, East Leake is one of the larger villages in south west Nottinghamshire — a rural area between the River Trent, the River Soar and an ancient roadway, the Fosse. It is situated between three major towns — Nottingham 10 miles to the north east, Derby 10 miles to the north west and Loughborough 6 miles to the south. It is in the area of the Borough Council of Rushcliffe.

The village is a local centre providing facilities for the nearby villages. There are shops, a health centre, a public library and a post office. The Harry Carlton Comprehensive School and Leisure Centre draws its support from the villages of south west Nottinghamshire and there are two primary schools for village children. St Mary's Church is the centre of a united benefice of the local churches of East Leake, West Leake, Costock, Rempstone and Stanford-on-Soar together with the Holy Cross Convent at Rempstone. The Baptist, Roman Catholic, Evangelical and Methodist churches all serve the surrounding area.

The most important industry is the mining and processing of gypsum. British Plaster Board, an international company, has one of its main centres at East Leake. There are minor industries and business concerns including the latest in communications and crop production.

The population is about 6000 people, many of whom commute to the local towns.

PART ONE — EARLY TIMES

Pre-history, new stone age, bronze age, iron/Romano age and Anglo-Saxon times, AD 410 - 900

There are no written records of man in Britain in early times. Nevertheless it is possible to build up the history of the area about East Leake by linking the accumulated knowledge of the past with artefacts, physical features and patterns of settlement in south west Nottinghamshire.

Before 4500 BC, man had led a nomadic existence relying on wild animals and plants to maintain himself and his domestic animals. He required trackways, setting them out along the ridges and streams. Many continue in use to this day and their courses can be traced. There were two major ridgeways in Leake. One, the Streetway, follows the ridge from Rempstone to Mill Hill in West Leake, and then along a ridge to the south side of the River Trent past Nottingham and Newark. At Moulter Hill there is a tumulus, an earthen mound raised to mark the route, and nearby Scotland Farm recalls a scot, a point used when tracks were surveyed. The other ridgeway, Portway, comes across from the Leicestershire Wolds and the Fosse to follow the ridge by the Rushcliffe golf course to the River Trent. The actual point of the crossing varied with changes in the course of the river.

There is a tumulus, the Cuckoo Bush between West Leake and Gotham. Cuckoos are reputed to have used the same breeding places since ancient times and about 23rd April each year, the first cuckoo can be heard at this point. It is reasonable to assume that, in the summer, man used the lowland tracks along the Kingston and Sheepwash Brooks (as they are now called).

In the new stone age man changed his way of life, clearing the forest to set up farmsteads to house his family and to cultivate crops. The Trent Valley was cleared at this time, as its gravel and sandy soils were suitable for cultivation with his primitive tools and ploughs. An adze, a stone implement for scraping wood, was found at a farm to the west of the village indicating an early settlement of man in the area about Leake. A collection of flint flakes was found in the field at the junction between the Portway and a track way from West Leake.

It is likely that in the several periods between 4500 BC and the iron age 1000 BC the Trent Valley was successively farmed. The recent discovery of a bronze age burial in Costock supports this view.

IRON AGE FARMING AND THE ROMAN OCCUPATION

During the iron age a Celtic tribe, the Coritani, settled in the East Midlands living there throughout the Roman occupation. Recent research suggests that this tribe should be called the Corieltavi. They were able people involved in farming, quarrying, mining and trade. Throughout the Roman occupation they continued to govern the East Midlands, gradually adopting Roman habits and customs. There is much evidence of intensive occupation of the area around East Leake, indeed throughout the valleys of the Trent, Derwent and Soar. Roman coins were discovered in East Leake when the Great Central Railway made a cutting across the Streetway.

In the area of south west Nottinghamshire it is possible to identify a group of farming estates, each consisting of several farms or homesteads under a "king" or leader who lived at a superior homestead or villa. The king provided security and organisation for trade in the surplus grain. Tessellated pavements have been found at Stanford-on-Soar, Barton-in-Fabis and Flawforth[1]. These were sites of villas and an estate can be envisaged about each of them. It is reasonable to

---

1. Today a lost settlement marked by the foundations of a Saxon church and graveyard near Ruddington.

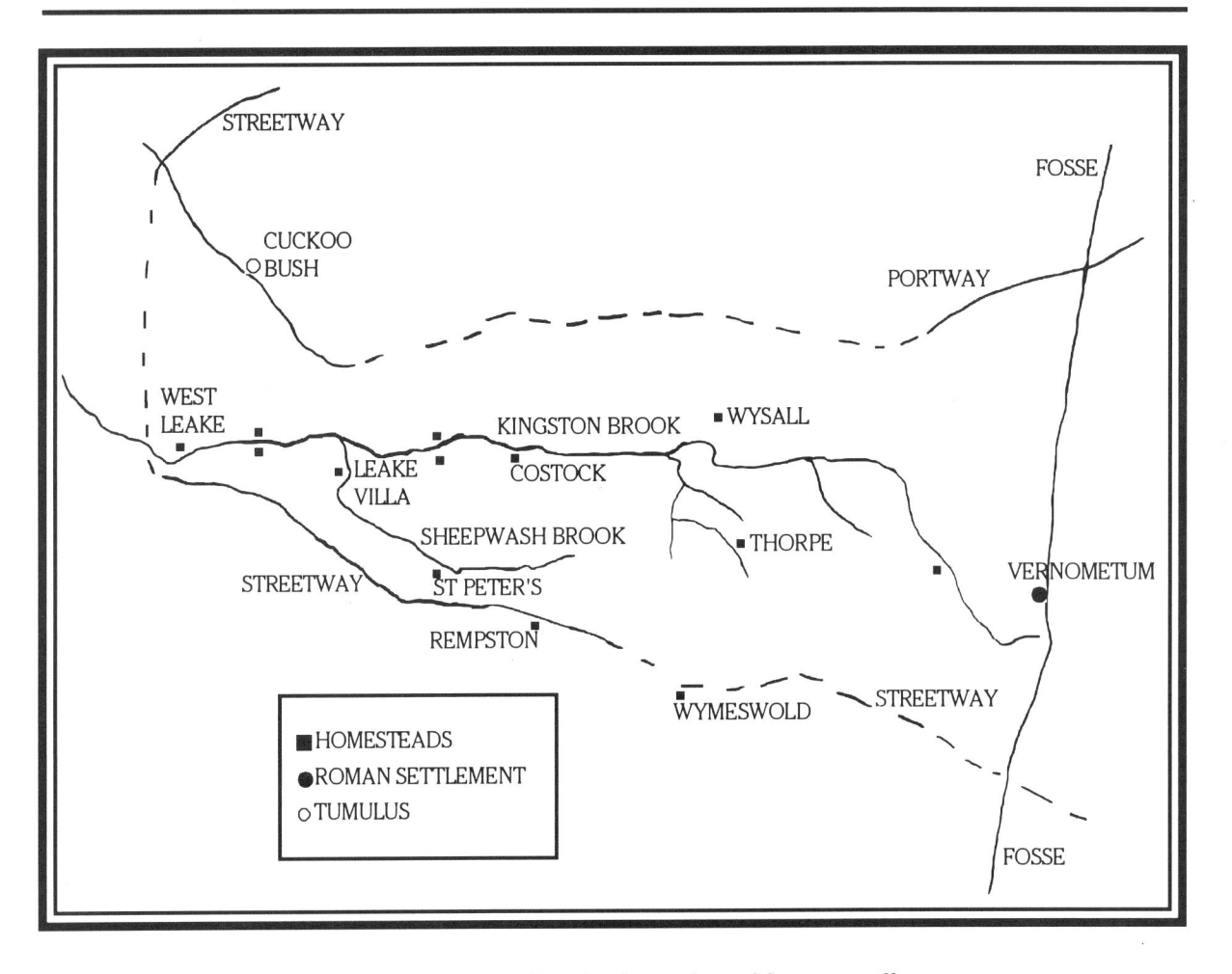

The iron age estate in East Leake and neighbouring villages

suppose that there was an estate along the Kingston and Sheepwash brooks with a villa probably on the present-day site of St Mary's church and with sites for farmsteads at Foxhill, St Peter's-in-the-Rushes, West Leake, Costock and even further along the brooks. These brooks were navigable and grain could be transported to the River Soar to supply the important town of Ratae (Leicester), to the River Trent for export to Europe and to the Fosse to supply the Roman garrison at Vernometum.

THE EARLY SAXON PERIOD AD 410 - 900

At the time of the withdrawal of the Romans in AD 410 the population was a mixture of the native Coritani and the Anglo-Saxons from Central Europe who had served in the Roman forces, staying here upon their discharge. During the next two centuries more Anglo Saxons came to England and these peoples became known as the English. Their settlements were consolidated into the kingdoms of Northumbria, East Anglia, Mercia and other smaller kingdoms.

Sometime during this period it is likely that settlements took place at Leake and they became known as Great or East Leake and Little or West Leake. Leche is the old English word for a water meadow. These were nucleated villages with the homesteads in a street with a leader or lord in the central homestead. The villagers would meet to conduct the business of the community – the basis of English democracy and the forerunner of the vestry and eventually the parish council.

Each would be a self-sufficing farming community, farming the land about the village and eventually adopting an open field system. At first there were two ploughed fields. In any one year one field would grow corn whilst the other would be fallowed, ie not cropped, then alternating from year to year. Later there was a change to a three field system with winter corn, spring corn and fallow in successive years. These fields were divided into strips. According to their status villagers were entitled to a number of strips. These would be allotted every year and scattered in the field. Villagers would not get the same strips every year. This distributed variations in the quality of the land, but prevented individual ownership and improvement. The fallow field, grassland, woodland and waste land would be grazed by cattle, sheep and pigs, with some of the grassland set aside for hay. The numbers of cattle, sheep and pigs and the strips in the hay field would be allotted to the villagers in accordance with their status.

Representation of the Saxon church at Esterleke showing how the present church might have looked in the early days. Drawn by David Clarke.

The Anglo-Saxons brought the north European system of government. This was a series of tiers from the king downward. At local level, groups of one hundred villages were formed into wapentakes or hundreds. Great or East Leake was in Rushcliffe and it was represented at a court which met on the Portway at Court Hill by the Cuckoo Bush. Little or West Leake was in the small Plumtree Hundred. The two villages have had their own administration, the parish vestry, and later the parish council ever since. The Catholic Church based its organisation on these parishes and the Church of England continued to do so after the Reformation by Henry VIII.

Little is known of local events during this period. Circa AD 600 Christian missionaries were sent out by Penda, King of Mercia, and it is likely that they came to Leake, preaching at the lord's homestead. Penda was a pagan with liberal views and his son was a Christian. Early Saxon quoins in the tower of St Mary's Church at East Leake indicate that there was a refuge tower by the lord's homestead from which they would have preached. The lord could have appointed a priest and built a simple church.

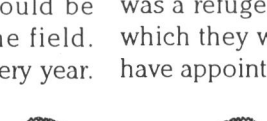

PART TWO — A MEDIEVAL AGRICULTURAL COMMUNITY

The coming of the Danes, Danelaw, Domesday, the medieval parish, the manors and the Leake family

The Danes had been coming to England from about AD 787. Some were primarily immigrants, trading and farming in the rich areas of southern England. Others came for political power, warring among themselves and against the English. Eventually they occupied Danelaw, an area north and east of a line from Chester to London along Watling Street. The East Midlands were relatively peaceful. At some time Danes settled in both Great and Little Leake, probably between AD 750 and 900.

By the eleventh century Great Leake was a township populated by freemen and villeins (villagers), most of them descendants of free Danish settlers. Domesday, the taxation record ordered by William the Conqueror in 1086, records two manors in the time of King Edward the Confessor (1065) one belonging to Siward and the other to Godric, both of whom were Danes. After the Norman Conquest, King William gave the chief manor to Henry de Ferrers and Godric's Manor to Roger of Bully. These two men were powerful and held many lands throughout the Midlands

Also there were two sokes, one being under the jurisdiction of the neighbouring manor of Gotham, part of the land of the Count of Mortain, and the other belonging to Stanford, part of the land of Robert, Son of King William. These two parcels of land remained in the ownership of the principal landowners in Stanford-on-Soar and Gotham. That in Stanford is mentioned in an indenture and claim (1461 - 1465) by which Richard Illingworth received the Manor of Stanford and several lands including some in both Great and Little Leek from Matilda (niece of Ralph, Lord Cromwell) and her husband Sir Gervase Clifton. This land may have been to the north of the Rempstone Road opposite Stanford Park. At the enclosure 1798 it was awarded to John Hollis and John Angrave. Later it was purchased by the Dashwoods, owners of Stanford Hall. The parcel belonging to Gotham appears in the enclosure as a small plot allotted to George Nathanial Curzon, a relation of the Howe family with lands in Gotham. It was in the middle of a large field now part of the Rushcliffe Golf Course.

At Domesday there were 38 persons recorded in Leche, a priest, Roger de Bully's man Ernulf, 18 freemen and 18 villagers. Persons without rights to land were not recorded. This suggests that there were over forty families. At the standard of five persons per family the total population can be estimated as over two hundred. Each family occupied a homestead and the plots on which they stood can still be identified on the enclosure plan of 1798 (page 27).

The freemen, or sokemen, were tenants of land, owing only light labour services to the lord. They were free, enjoyed a degree of independence and were responsible for the discharge of taxation on their lands. Some may have been involved in activities other than farming, such as weaving or trading.

The villagers or villeins were peasants with a toft and croft, ie the house and buildings of a homestead and a piece of land, or close. They were free, but owed labour service on the lord's demesne or home farm, working two to three days per week and seasonal work in addition.

Whilst the overall jurisdiction would have been by the tenants in chief, the de Ferrers and the Bullys, the freemen and villagers conducted the day-to-day business as a vestry which met at the church.

Leche at this time must have been a township of importance in south west Nottinghamshire, on a par with Plumtree and Flawforth (Ruddington).

A new church was built about the middle of the eleventh century and dedicated to St Leonard. This was a minster or mother church where there was a priest responsible for the masses at his church and those in the neighbouring villages, probably Costock, Rempstone, Little Leche and Stanford. There is evidence of late Saxon and early Norman work in all of these churches.

The chief manor of Leke held by Henry de Ferrers included an outlier or berewick in the jurisdiction

4	Land of the Count of Mortain (Rushcliffe Wapentake)	282d
4	In Leake 2b of land taxable. Nothing there. Jurisdiction of this manor (Gotham)	
9	Land of Roger of Bully (In Rushcliffe Wapentake)	284c
89M	In Leake Godric had 2b of land and the third part of 1b taxable. Land for 4 oxen. Ernulf, Roger's man, has 2 ploughs and 2 villagers with ½ plough. Meadow, 8 acres. Value before 1066, 40 s: now 10 s.	
24	Land of Henry of Ferrers (Rushcliffe Wapentake)	291d
1M	In Leake Siward had 2c of land taxable. Land for 6 ploughs. Henry of Ferrers has in lordship 4 ploughs and 16 freemen and 16 villagers who have 17 ploughs. A priest and a church; 1 mill, 2 s; meadow 50 acres; underwood 2 furlongs long and 1 wide. Value before 1066 £6: now £7. To this manor is attached the outlier of Leake where there are 2c of land taxable. It lies in Plumtree Hundred.	
28	(Land) of Robert Son of William	292a
2S	In Stanton, Leake 1b of land taxable. Land for 4 oxen. 2 Freemen have 1 plough. It belongs to Stanford.	

Domesday Book 25 Nottinghamshire, John Morris 1977, Phillimore & Co Ltd, London and Chichester

Bovate — an eighth of a carucate
Carucate — a unit of land measurement in Danish areas which is about 125 acres

The entries for Leake extracted from the Domesday Book, 1086

of Plumtree Hundred. Domesday does not give any further information about this outlier, a typical omission. However, Thoroton identifies it as Little Leake or West Leake. This was a small village with a manor awarded to Jordan de Toc, a Norman in the service of Henry de Ferrers, Master of the Horse of William the Conqueror at the Battle of Hastings.

A PICTURE OF THE MEDIEVAL PARISH

The bounds of the parish had been formed by the start of the twelfth century. Most of the boundaries were physical features and were almost, if not quite, the same as today (map page 31). Streamlets, or sics as they are called, account for some three quarters of the total boundary. On the western side, there is a length along the top of a cliff or escarpment, and in the south-east corner the ancient Streetway has been used. The south end of the western boundary between Great and Little Leake has been drawn by man.

The Kingston Brook flows from the east to west through the centre of the parish. The main street is to the south above flood level. The map shows over thirty plots on either side of the main street and village green – they can be identified still. It is reasonable to assume that the homesteads of the eighteen freemen and eighteen villagers were located on these plots at the time of Domesday.

The village green was at the west end of the main street, the Sheepwash Brook flowing through it from the south to join the Kingston Brook. The church and the chief manor house, later called Shirley's Manor and today Old Hall Farm, were on the west bank with an undershot water mill nearby. The manor awarded to Roger de Bully, known as Joyce's Manor and today as Brookside Farm, was on the Sheepwash Brook to the west of the green.

At the east end of the main street there was a crossroads between the Portway and the Streetway. There was a high point, probably the site of a castle, a stockaded enclosure built during the troubled times of the reign of King Stephen (1135 - 1154). The parish constable's accounts between 1791 and 1835 record repairs to the chimneys, chamber and windows of the castle and for thatch. This house has not been identified but there is a cruck[2] cottage by the site. Also in this area there was a Borough Pool for the supply of fish.

The three open fields spread beyond the brooks and main street. The map shows them as they are identified by the enclosure award. The medieval fields were much smaller and there is physical evidence of this in Woodgate Field to the south of the main street where, in the twelfth century, the ridge and furrows extended from the homesteads to the top of the hill and the ploughs turned to create a slight bank. Subsequently this open field was extended down to the stream beyond and the ridge and furrows can be seen as continuous from the street to the stream, ie the ploughs went over the banks.

Woodgate Field occupied the whole of the south-western corner of the parish southward from the meadows along the Kingston Brook and the main street to the southern boundary, a sic flowing westwardly from the Lings Common.

Hill Field spread north-west from the Kingston Brook meadows on the lower lying gravels to the foothills at the north of the parish.

Brickcliffe Field was on the eastern side of the parish, divided into two parts by the Kingston Brook.

Access from the village to the open fields was off the ancient trackways, Normanton Lane, Old West Leake Road, Sheep Plank Lane and the Crossroad and by short lanes from Main Street, Poke Lane (now Station Road), The Nook and Gotham Lane.

Westward the land rises steeply to the parish boundary – this hillside was common grazing. More northerly the soil is a boulder clay, not so suitable for ploughing. This was under grass for grazing and mowing – Risely Common, Hotchley or High Field, The Moors, Hooping or Lime Kiln Common and Lammas Close. On the lower land on the Gotham side there were the hay fields, Welldale, where the villagers were allotted rights to cut hay. The eastern boundary of the parish from its more northerly point is a sic with common grazing and rough scrub on the lowland side.

In the south-eastern corner of the parish and extending into Rempstone and Stanford there is an area of gravel on the higher lands known as the Lings. This land was very suitable for sheep and in the fifteenth century the rector kept a large flock of sheep. The village, the manor and the church of St Peter-in-the-Rushes were in the middle of this area.

---

2. Cruck: Pairs of large timbers inclined inwards from the line of the outer wall to the apex to support the ridge beam

THE LEAKE FAMILY AND THE CHIEF MANOR

In the middle of the eleventh century, a free Danish settler, Alan, came to Leche and called himself Alan of Leche or Lake. This was an event which was to have a great influence on Leche for his descendants were to be the lords of the chief manor for the next six hundred years, when they sold them to the Armstrongs of Rempstone. They held lands in both Great and Little Leake throughout this period and the manor house, known today as Old Hall Farm, was to the north of St Mary's church.

Harold of Lake, Alan's son, was an important steward of the Earl of Chester who had authority over much of the Midlands.

A deed of 1140 records the passing of the Leake lands to his son Alan de Leca.

"Robert de Ferraris, Grandchild of Henry before named, Earl of Nottingham, gave to Alan de Leca, the nephew of Elfast, the Town of Leche, where the Mother Church is with all the appurtenances, and twelve Bovates of Land in this the said Earl's, which were the said Alan's parents and in Stanton as much as belonged to the said Earls fee, and divers other lands in the County of Leicester, for which the said Alan gave the Earl fifty marks and a certain bay (Baucham) Horse."

"The said Alan's parents" referred to his father Harold.

Alan had two sons, Henricus (Henry) whose descendants held the Leake manor and Harold whose descendants held the Staunton Harold manor, near Breedon, Leicestershire, and took the name "de Staunton".

From the twelfth century the chief manor of Great Leake passed in the direct line of eldest sons from Henricus to a Sir Alan of Leake who died without heir in 1362. His father, Sir John, had died of plague in 1359. Following Sir Alan's death the Leake manors seem to have passed to his uncle, Thomas, Lord of the Manor of Cotham in Nottinghamshire. His heir was Sir Alan's younger brother, Sir John Leeke who had two sons. The elder, Simon, died young and the younger, another John, succeeded to the manors and extensive lands of the family at Cotham and Leake. By his first wife he added lands in Lincolnshire. About 1400 he married his second wife, Alicia Grey of Sandiacre, heiress to the Derbyshire estates of the Greys at Sandicliffe and Sutton Scarsdale. Their son William died in 1458 and his son, John the Elder, was only eight years old when he inherited the considerable lands of his grandfather. He was the first of the Leake family to live at Sutton Scarsdale.

This branch of the Leakes continued to live at Sutton Scarsdale and enlarged the mansion and church there. The rest of the family spread into Norfolk, Nottinghamshire, Derbyshire and the Midlands.

Sir Francis Leek supported the King during the Civil War (1641 - 47) and was awarded the barony of Deincourt, later becoming Earl of Scarsdale. Cromwell sequestrated his estates but they were returned by Charles II.

Sir Francis Leek the younger, (1549 - 1626) had spent lavishly on extending the mansion at Scarsdale to make it one of the largest in Derbyshire. He overspent and the Leake lands were acquired by Sir Robert Shirley of Staunton Harold. The Leake Manor then became known as Shirley's manor. Sir Robert Shirley was a descendant of Harold of Staunton. In 1422 his descendant, John of Staunton, died and his sole heir, Margaret, married Ralph Shirley, a distant relative of her mother, Joan Meynell. This brought together the estates of the Stauntons and the Shirleys, a family descended from Sewaldus, an Old Englishman who had come from Northern Europe, probably in the ninth or tenth century and settled at Shirley near Ashbourne in Derbyshire. Sir Robert Shirley was very rich, his mother being co-heir of the 11th Earl Ferrers, 2nd Earl of Essex. He built Staunton Harold Church in the Anglican tradition as a gesture against the Commonwealth. Sir Robert's son, Robert, revived the title of Earl Ferrers and his descendants continued to live at Staunton Harold until the twentieth century.

In the twelfth century the Lordship of the Manor of Little Leake was held by the Tocs, passing successively to the Bugges, Manners and Harwars until in 1594 a Leake, Richard Mansfield exchanged his manor at Caunton near Newark for that of Little Leake. A branch of the Leake family had established itself at Caunton earlier and Richard's memorial in St Helena's Church at Little Leake includes the arms of both Leake (annulets) and Shirley (ermine)

The spread of the families from Alan of Lecke, Sewaldus, Shirley and Henry de Ferrers has been very wide. Bess of Hardwick was a near relative of the Leakes. Mary Leake married a Markham, an extensive family in north Nottinghamshire of which there are some descendants today.

It is strange that no memorial to a Leake remains in St Mary's Church at Great Leake. It is possible that memorials and tombs were despoiled during the Reformation and any markings were lost when the chancel was rebuilt in 1866. There are three tombs in St Helena's Church at Little Leake, all dating to the twelfth century. The figure on the tomb in the vestry has annulets on the robe, identifying it as a Leake, possibly Robert, grandson of Henricus.

From the seventeenth century Leakes emigrated to America and to Australia. From time to time American Leakes visit East and West Leake, their ancestral home. One, Preston H Leake, has published the results of his research into the Leakes of Virginia, some of whom were involved in the development of tobacco estates and industry. He lists over nine thousand Leakes who have lived or are living in Virginia and mentions a tobacco estate called Shirley.

The Leakes have left little evidence of their riches in East and West Leake. The Saxon and the twelfth century parts of St Mary's Church at East Leake can be attributed to them. Early in the twelfth century Harold of Leke made a substantial alteration to his church at Leake replacing the south wall of the nave with an Early English arcade and south aisle, inserting large Early English arches at each end of the nave, raising the roof and enlarging the chancel. Carved heads on the two easterly pillars of the arcade could be those of Harold and his wife. The inclusion of the Leake arms on the east window of the chancel at West Leake, noted by Thoroton, indicates that it was built by a Leake. Little of their houses has been identified. Until recently parts of an aisled timber-framed building opposite the north door of St Mary's Church at East Leake could have been the remnants of an early manor house of the Leakes. It was unfortunate that the timbers were not fully recorded and dated before this was pulled down.

Around 1100 Harold of Leke was involved with the Earl of Chester in building the village and church at Calke in south Derbyshire, some twelve miles west of Leake. In 1104 he was appointed by Robert de Ferrers and the Earl of Chester to raise the funds and organise the work of building one of the earliest Augustinian priories there. The priory housed twelve canons. As Lord of the Manor of Leke Harold gave to the priory one carucate (125 acres) of land in Leke and three acres of meadow in the Town of Leke. At the same time he gave the advowson[3] of Leke to the canons together with the tithes for their maintenance in perpetuity. The priory became a cell of Repton Priory in 1160 but the advowson and tithes continued to maintain the canons at Calke until its dissolution in 1537. Today the link between Calke and Leake is marked by Calke Hall, an outlying farm homestead on the Streetway between East and West Leake.

The first rector of Leake, William Leke, was presented in 1206, and he was the only Leake to have been rector of the Church of Leake.

In 1415 a manor had been split from the chief manor and awarded to Roger Pare, son of Ralph. His son died without male heir and his daughter, Isabel, wife of Robert Cosby, inherited this manor and it became known as Cosby's Manor. The homestead was on the south side of the main street to the west of the Bulls Head and was demolished when Salisbury Avenue was developed in 1963. Richard, grandson of Isabel, succeeded to this manor on her death in 1543. Later it was acquired by the Armstrongs of Rempstone who subsequently sold it with their other Leake properties to Sir Thomas Parkyns of Bunny.

The early history of the manor awarded to Roger de Bully has not been traced. In 1331 a deed includes a reference to Robert de Jorce Knt (generally spelt Joyce) settling on Sir John Leeke, Parson of Humberstone, and his heirs several parcels of land in Esterleke. This suggests that the Jorce family, with lands at Wymeswold, Leicestershire, and Burton Joyce, Nottinghamshire, had acquired the manor awarded to de Bully.

In the seventeenth to eighteenth century Joyce's Manor was a stone house to the west of the Sheepwash Brook in the possession of the Bleys and Hardys.

---

3. Advowson: The right of recommending a member of the Anglican clergy for a vacant benefice.

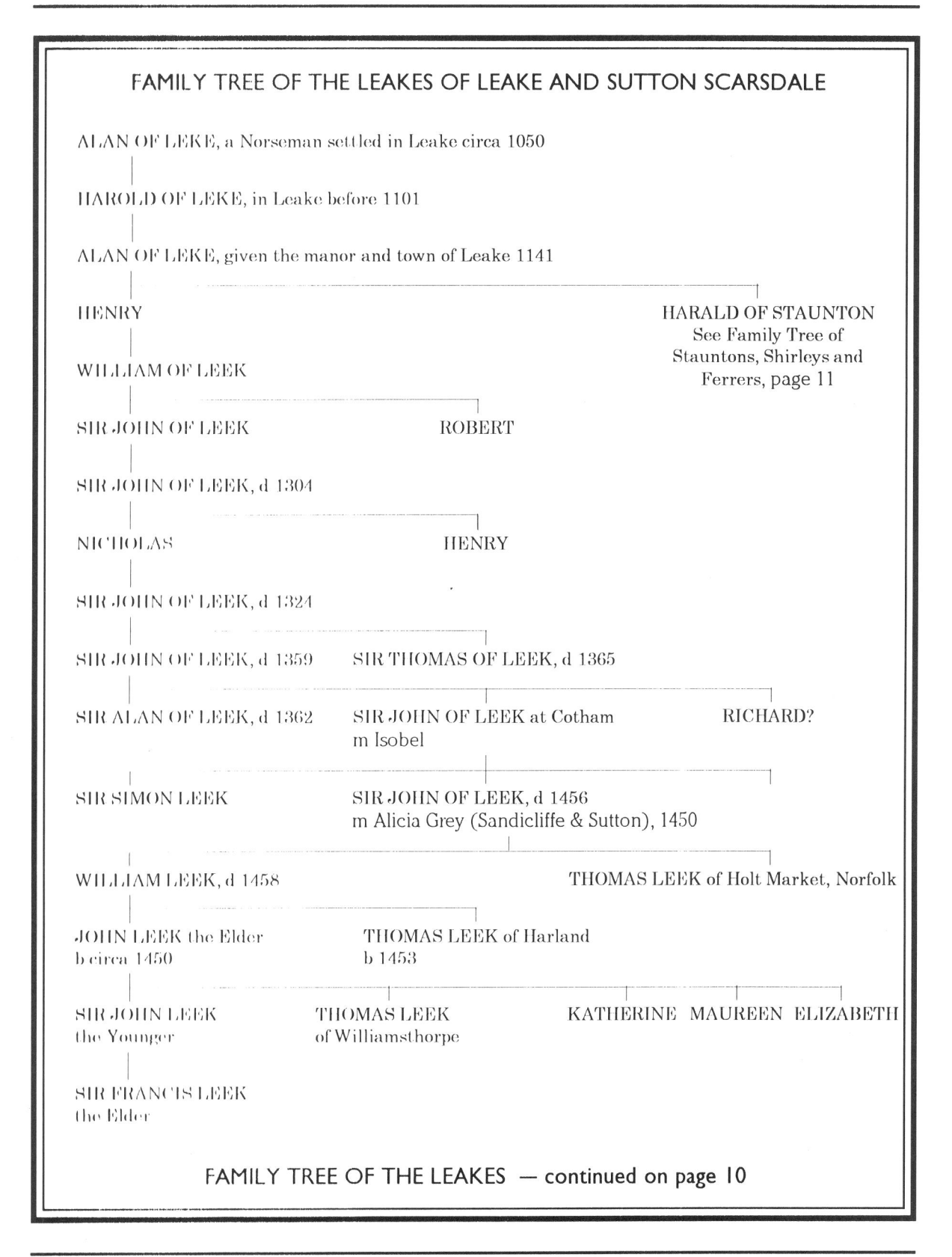

FAMILY TREE OF THE LEAKES OF LEAKE AND SUTTON SCARSDALE

ALAN OF LEKE, a Norseman settled in Leake circa 1050
|
HAROLD OF LEKE, in Leake before 1101
|
ALAN OF LEKE, given the manor and town of Leake 1141
|
|--|
HENRY   HARALD OF STAUNTON
| See Family Tree of
| Stauntons, Shirleys and
WILLIAM OF LEEK   Ferrers, page 11
|
|--------------------------------|
SIR JOHN OF LEEK   ROBERT
|
SIR JOHN OF LEEK, d 1304
|
|--------------------------------|
NICHOLAS   HENRY
|
SIR JOHN OF LEEK, d 1324
|
|--------------------------------|
SIR JOHN OF LEEK, d 1359   SIR THOMAS OF LEEK, d 1365
| |
| |---------------------------------|
SIR ALAN OF LEEK, d 1362   SIR JOHN OF LEEK at Cotham   RICHARD?
| m Isobel
| |
SIR SIMON LEEK   SIR JOHN OF LEEK, d 1456
                                 m Alicia Grey (Sandicliffe & Sutton), 1450
                                 |
                                 |---------------------------------|
| |
WILLIAM LEEK, d 1458   THOMAS LEEK of Holt Market, Norfolk
|
|--------------------------------|
JOHN LEEK the Elder   THOMAS LEEK of Harland
b circa 1450   b 1453
|
|------------------|-----------------|----------------|---------------|
SIR JOHN LEEK   THOMAS LEEK   KATHERINE   MAUREEN   ELIZABETH
the Younger   of Williamsthorpe
|
SIR FRANCIS LEEK
the Elder

FAMILY TREE OF THE LEAKES — continued on page 10

FAMILY TREE OF THE LEAKES — continued from page 9

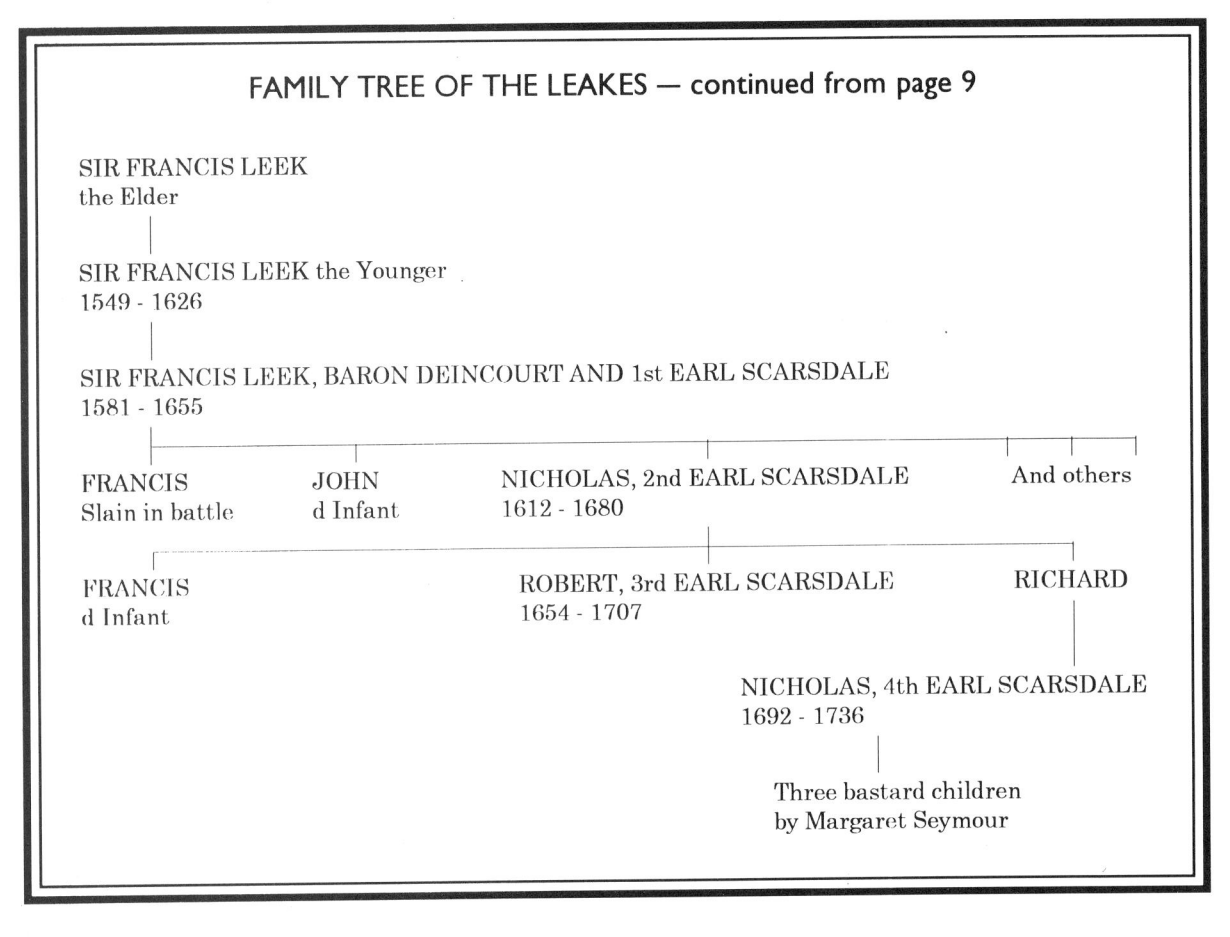

SIR FRANCIS LEEK
the Elder
|
SIR FRANCIS LEEK the Younger
1549 - 1626
|
SIR FRANCIS LEEK, BARON DEINCOURT AND 1st EARL SCARSDALE
1581 - 1655

FRANCIS	JOHN	NICHOLAS, 2nd EARL SCARSDALE	And others
Slain in battle	d Infant	1612 - 1680	

FRANCIS	ROBERT, 3rd EARL SCARSDALE	RICHARD
d Infant	1654 - 1707	

NICHOLAS, 4th EARL SCARSDALE
1692 - 1736
|
Three bastard children
by Margaret Seymour

Family Tree of the Leakes of Leake and Sutton Scarsdale

FAMILY TREE OF STAUNTONS, SHIRLEYS AND FERRERS

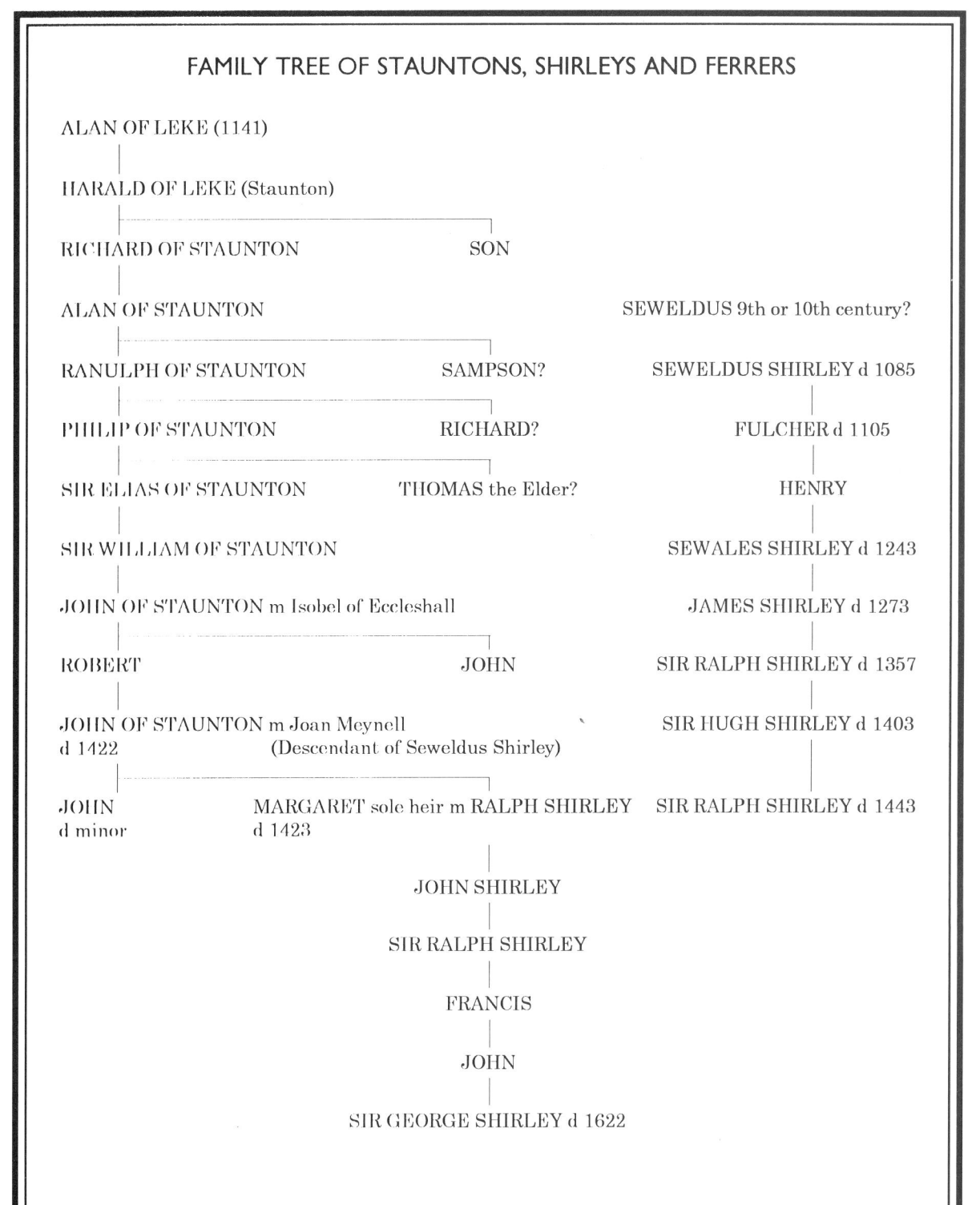

ALAN OF LEKE (1141)
|
HARALD OF LEKE (Staunton)
|
|---------------------------|
RICHARD OF STAUNTON   SON
|
ALAN OF STAUNTON   SEWELDUS 9th or 10th century?
RANULPH OF STAUNTON   SAMPSON?   SEWELDUS SHIRLEY d 1085
PHILIP OF STAUNTON   RICHARD?   FULCHER d 1105
SIR ELIAS OF STAUNTON   THOMAS the Elder?   HENRY
SIR WILLIAM OF STAUNTON   SEWALES SHIRLEY d 1243
JOHN OF STAUNTON m Isobel of Eccleshall   JAMES SHIRLEY d 1273
ROBERT   JOHN   SIR RALPH SHIRLEY d 1357
JOHN OF STAUNTON m Joan Meynell   SIR HUGH SHIRLEY d 1403
d 1422   (Descendant of Seweldus Shirley)
JOHN   MARGARET sole heir m RALPH SHIRLEY   SIR RALPH SHIRLEY d 1443
d minor   d 1423
JOHN SHIRLEY
SIR RALPH SHIRLEY
FRANCIS
JOHN
                   SIR GEORGE SHIRLEY d 1622

FAMILY TREE OF STAUNTONS, SHIRLEYS AND FERRERS — continued on page 12

FAMILY TREE OF STAUNTONS, SHIRLEYS AND FERRERS — continued from page 11

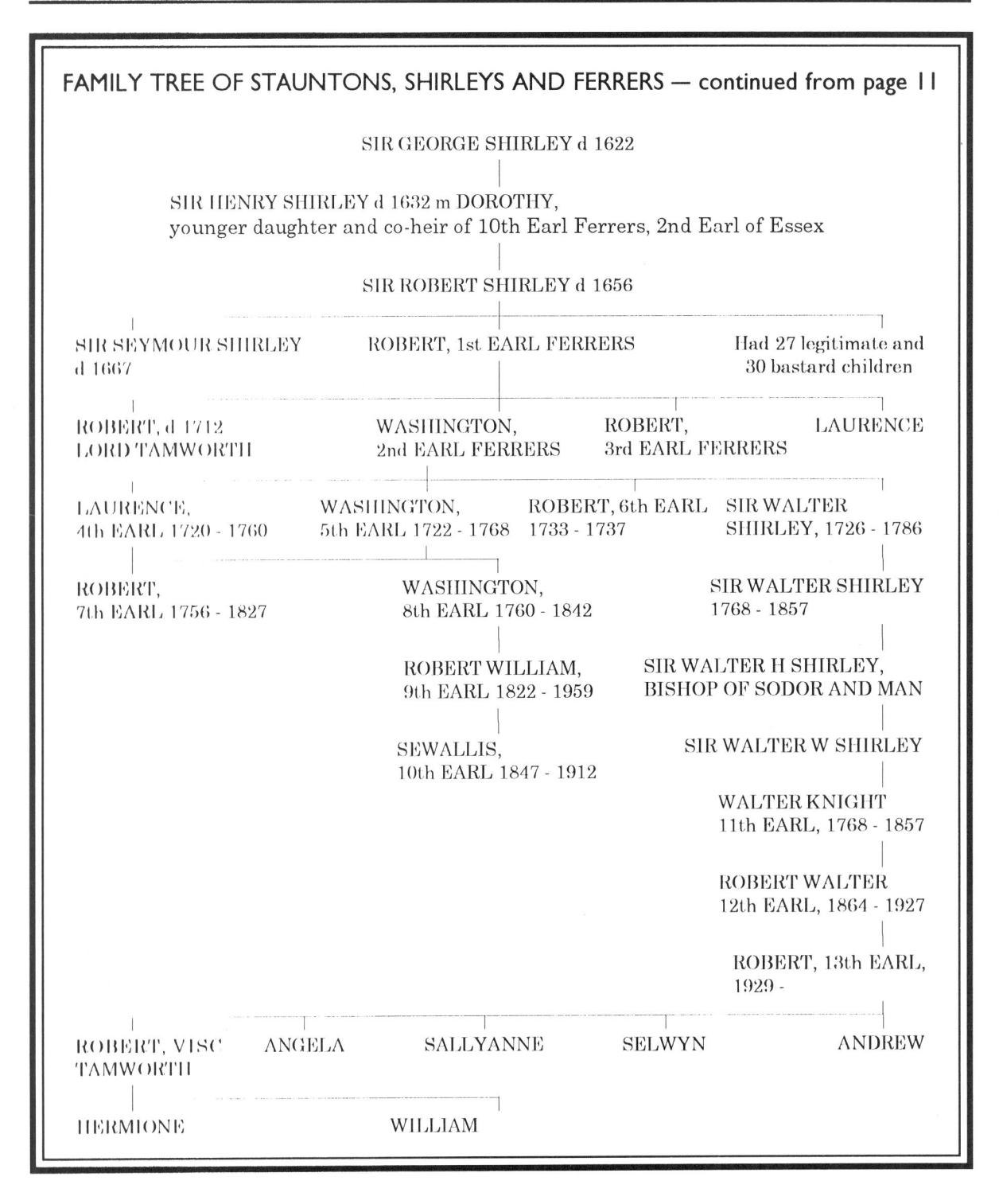

SIR GEORGE SHIRLEY d 1622

SIR HENRY SHIRLEY d 1632 m DOROTHY,
younger daughter and co-heir of 10th Earl Ferrers, 2nd Earl of Essex

SIR ROBERT SHIRLEY d 1656

| SIR SEYMOUR SHIRLEY d 1667 | ROBERT, 1st EARL FERRERS | Had 27 legitimate and 30 bastard children |

| ROBERT, d 1712 LORD TAMWORTH | WASHINGTON, 2nd EARL FERRERS | ROBERT, 3rd EARL FERRERS | LAURENCE |

| LAURENCE, 4th EARL 1720 - 1760 | WASHINGTON, 5th EARL 1722 - 1768 | ROBERT, 6th EARL 1733 - 1737 | SIR WALTER SHIRLEY, 1726 - 1786 |

| ROBERT, 7th EARL 1756 - 1827 | WASHINGTON, 8th EARL 1760 - 1842 | | SIR WALTER SHIRLEY 1768 - 1857 |

ROBERT WILLIAM, 9th EARL 1822 - 1959

SIR WALTER H SHIRLEY, BISHOP OF SODOR AND MAN

SEWALLIS, 10th EARL 1847 - 1912

SIR WALTER W SHIRLEY

WALTER KNIGHT 11th EARL, 1768 - 1857

ROBERT WALTER 12th EARL, 1864 - 1927

ROBERT, 13th EARL, 1929 -

| ROBERT, VISC TAMWORTH | ANGELA | SALLYANNE | SELWYN | ANDREW |

| HERMIONE | WILLIAM |

Family Tree of Stauntons, Shirleys and Ferrers

PART THREE — THIRTEENTH TO EIGHTEENTH CENTURIES

A medieval community, the Treaty of Leake, local administration, the yeomen, the Town Lands Trust, John Bley, occupations, the Church and non-conformity

THE TOWN OF GREAT LEAKE – A MEDIEVAL COMMUNITY

For much of the medieval period, Great Leake was a leading township in south west Nottinghamshire although following the Leakes there was no rich landowner resident in East Leake. Parkyns lived at Bunny and Bley was in London. But throughout the medieval period there was a group of affluent families — the yeomen (farmers), landowners, grocers, shepherds and tradesmen. There was every indication of a flourishing community.

During this time the Town of Great Leake was a community of some two hundred and fifty to three hundred people living in about fifty homesteads. The upper class were the gentry, and their families, the Leakes and the Joyces.

The freemen of Domesday evolved to the middle class, mostly the yeomen and farmers. Over three hundred years later the twenty three land owners and tenants recorded as frank pledgemen were under the mutual bond of frank pledge for the conduct of the community. The families of the yeomen would amount to about one hundred people. The rest of the population included the families of the villagers together with the retainers and servants of the gentry and yeomen.

Great Leake was a duchy town under the administration of the Royal Duchy of Lancaster. It had privileges and marketing rights. Even as late as 1661 the bailiff of Loughborough arrested Richard Patrick's sack of corn for toll and the lords of the manors of Great and Little Leake commenced a suit against Loughborough on the grounds that East Leake was a duchy town and should be toll-free. The suit was dropped on the grounds of its high cost.

THE TREATY OF LEAKE

Throughout medieval times the town was a peaceful community, primarily involved in farming and rarely involved in national affairs.

However, in 1317 - 18 Leake became the scene of national event. The King, Edward II, and his powerful cousin Thomas, Earl of Lancaster, son of Edmund, were in disagreement over affairs of state and the Pope encouraged the nobility and cardinals to settle these differences. Leake was a convenient place to meet. Thomas controlled the duchy and had castles at Leicester and Castle Donington. His bailiff was Sir John Leek of Great Leake and Cardinal de Fargis, the rector of Leake, was a man in close contact with the Pope.

Meetings were arranged at Great Leake and Leicester. Doubtless there would have been a tented camp on the homesteads of either Great or Little Leake manor.

In the summer of 1318 the King had assembled a large army of some 18,000 men at Hathern. He stayed at Leake for four days either with Sir John Leek, or with Robert Touk of Little Leake Manor, collector of scutage (funds) in Derbyshire for the maintenance of his army in Scotland. On the 7th August, the King and Thomas Lancaster met at Zouch by Hathern and made their peace. Two days later they sealed their agreement at Great Leake and this became known as the Treaty of Leake.

LOCAL ADMINISTRATION

The duchy exercised local control through courts composed of the lords of the manors and juries of frank pledgemen, ie the landowners and tenants. The business of the Great Leake (Esterleek) courts was recorded in the rolls of the Honours of Tutbury and Tickhill in Derbyshire, the local administrative bodies of the Rushcliffe Hundred. The earlier courts were held under Tutbury but they changed to Tickhill in the sixteenth century when the lord of the principal manor, a Leek, was resident at Sutton Scarsdale in North Derbyshire (see pp 7 and 10).

Thus at a court on 3rd October 1406 there were twelve frank pledgemen present: Willm atte Mylne, John Wright, Hugh Brette, Edward Fraunkileyne, John Taillour, Thomas de Hul, Robert Stevendone, Peter of Gotham, John Smythe Senr, Simon of Cleybrook, John Banastre, John Smythe Junr and the following eleven were fined for non-attendance: John Humberstone of Leek Magna, Robert in le Vree of the same, Wm Aleyn of the same, John Fleccher of the same, John Aleyn of the same, John Stevensone of the same . . . Walter Garton of the same Leek, Hugh Prokator, Richd del Wroo, Simon Thomasone, Margerote . . .

In the time of Elizabeth I the chief pledgeman was William Burrowes (Barrow). His descendants were prominent landowners for the next three centuries. Another person mentioned was Richard Sheffield, a free tenant in 1566. His descendants, mainly shepherds and husbandmen, lived in the village into the twentieth century.

The workings of these courts can be shown by extracts from some fifteenth century rolls. Fines were imposed at 2d for each occasion on which they brewed beer without the knowledge of the lord or his servants on the following: John Leget 2d once, John Smyth 24d twelve times, Simon Claybrooke 8d four times, Richard Beall 8d four times, Alice Diepe 4d twice, and Richard Allbroo 8d four times. A chicken was found stray worth 2d.

At a court on 24th November 1411 fines were imposed for brewing and selling beer. Strays and the profit of strays were due to the lord of the manor – a stray swarm of bees was sold for 12 pence. At the mercy of the court were John Pope who assaulted Richard Cook, hayward of the sheep and Richard Valeyman fined 6d for drawing blood from Robert Gentyll. John Hunte, bailiff, was due 12d for one weakly and stray bullock. At a court on 26th April 1412 the high street was reported as muddy by default of the village and was to be amended before the next court.

Detailed records such as modern census returns and church registers are not available for the earlier medieval periods but it is possible to identify some yeomen and their properties. Potter's History of East Leake lists some landowners and their lands in the thirteenth and fourteenth centuries. In 1209 Reginald de Cardoil disposed of three virgates and 22 acres (112 acres in all). In 1270 Hugh Wake had a knight's fee of more than 100 acres, sufficient to maintain himself and a retinue. In 1280 John Beningworth claimed that as a landowner he had the right of patronage to the rectory. In the fourteenth century Richard de Pottiler had eight messuages and five virgates (150 acres), William Umfrey and Henry Green had lands.

THE HOMESTEADS AND THE YEOMEN

A few homesteads of the early medieval period have survived to the present time.

Across the brook from the east end of the church there is a timber-framed house, an example of those belonging to the better-off yeomen. This is a hall, ie a single room with a solarium, an upper floor to which the family retired. There would have been a central hearth, the smoke from which went through an opening in the roof. This building has not been dated but it is obviously the home of a yeoman of substance, maybe one of the Umfreys mentioned in the fifteenth century court rolls.

Most of the houses consisted of a single room, some 16 feet (5 metres) square. Those belonging to the yeomen were likely to have been cruck houses with service buildings such as dairies or livestock sheds whilst those of the servants were simple timber, wattle and daub buildings. These houses could be erected quickly by the family, were easily destroyed by fire or storm and rebuilt in a day. Two cruck houses have survived. One is about 100 metres from Joyce's Manor, now Brookside Farm. The other is in the area of the castle and adjacent to the farm house of the Oldershaws. About 1800 the constable's accounts record expenditure on the castle – maybe this cruck house. A third cruck was part of Ryholm Farm which was demolished in 1967. This was the property of the Woottons, yeomen in the seventeenth century.

Farming was flourishing in Elizabethan times (late sixteenth century). The yeomen rebuilt their homesteads. The farmhouses of this period were timber-framed with brick infills. Cellars are a feature of several of them, and these are associated with the affluent families, Burrowes, Hardy, Woodroffe and Wootton. There are ancient cellars at both Shirley's and Joyce's manors.

The typical Elizabethan farmhouse consisted of a single bay, 16 x 16 ft (4.9 x 4.9 m) hall and upper floor with an adjoining brick building for livestock and farming activities. They were mainly on Brookside and in the Nook. The Bleys and Hardys were associated with Brookside Farm (with cellar). The vicarage (Old Rectory) is described in the Terrier of Glebe Lands and Great Tithe of East Leake 1748. The Marcers were associated with one of four in the Nook. On Castle Hill the Bosworths had a thatched timber-framed house which was demolished in the twentieth century. Some have survived and others have been replaced with brick houses built on the original Elizabethan foundations.

In 1714 - 1728 John Bley built a new house with cellar in Main Street and called it Joyce's Manor. At the same time Sir Thomas Parkyns was building a mansion near to Shirley's Manor. It was never fully occupied and was pulled down, a source of materials for local houses and the walls of the graveyard and pinfold. Parkyns built a number of houses on his estates in south-west Nottinghamshire, but in Great Leake there is only one which has features in his style. This is a house with cellar in Station Road, occupied by the Woodroffes and extended by them about 1800.

During the eighteenth century farming continued to flourish. Some yeomen extended their timber-framed houses by adding bays and an upper storey in traditional timber framing or in brick. Others, Woottons at Ryholm and Burrows at Home Farm, replaced their old houses with two-storey brick houses. In the latter half of this century there was an increase in house building by the smaller farmers, by tradespeople, and by those engaged in lace and hosiery.

THE TOWN LANDS TRUST

In the sixteenth century central government moved to make it a legal obligation to relieve the poor by the levying of poor rates. An act of 1572 (the 14th Elizabeth C5) decreed that all should pay for this. In 1597 the overseers of the poor were the two church wardens and four householders.

In Great Leake a decree in the High Court of Chancery at Westminster on 21st November in the eleventh year of the reign of King Charles I (1637) set up the Town Lands Trust by which lands known as the Kirk Headland, the Town Land and the Common Meadow were to be employed for the General Good and Ease of the inhabitants of Great Leake. These lands were passed by Thomas and Richard Patrick to the Trustees, the two lords of the principal manors of Great and Little Leke, Gabriel Armstrong and Richard Mansfield, the Rector of Leke, the Reverend Edward Bigland and six yeomen or principal landowners: Richard Sheffield the eldest, George Wight, Richard North, Richard Yerwood, Henry Burrows and Richard Knott.

A deed appointing new trustees dated 1808 lists all the trustees between 1637 and 1808. They were yeomen, heirs and relatives of the original six yeomen trustees. In 1761 William North was a sole surviving trustee and he received five shillings from the new trustees in recognition of his work in managing the trust. This deed records that the enclosure award of 1798 allotted Plot 12, 21 acres and 33 perches to the trustees of the Town Lands for their lands and rights in Great Leke. Plot 22, 2 acres 3 roods 23 perches, was taken from them and

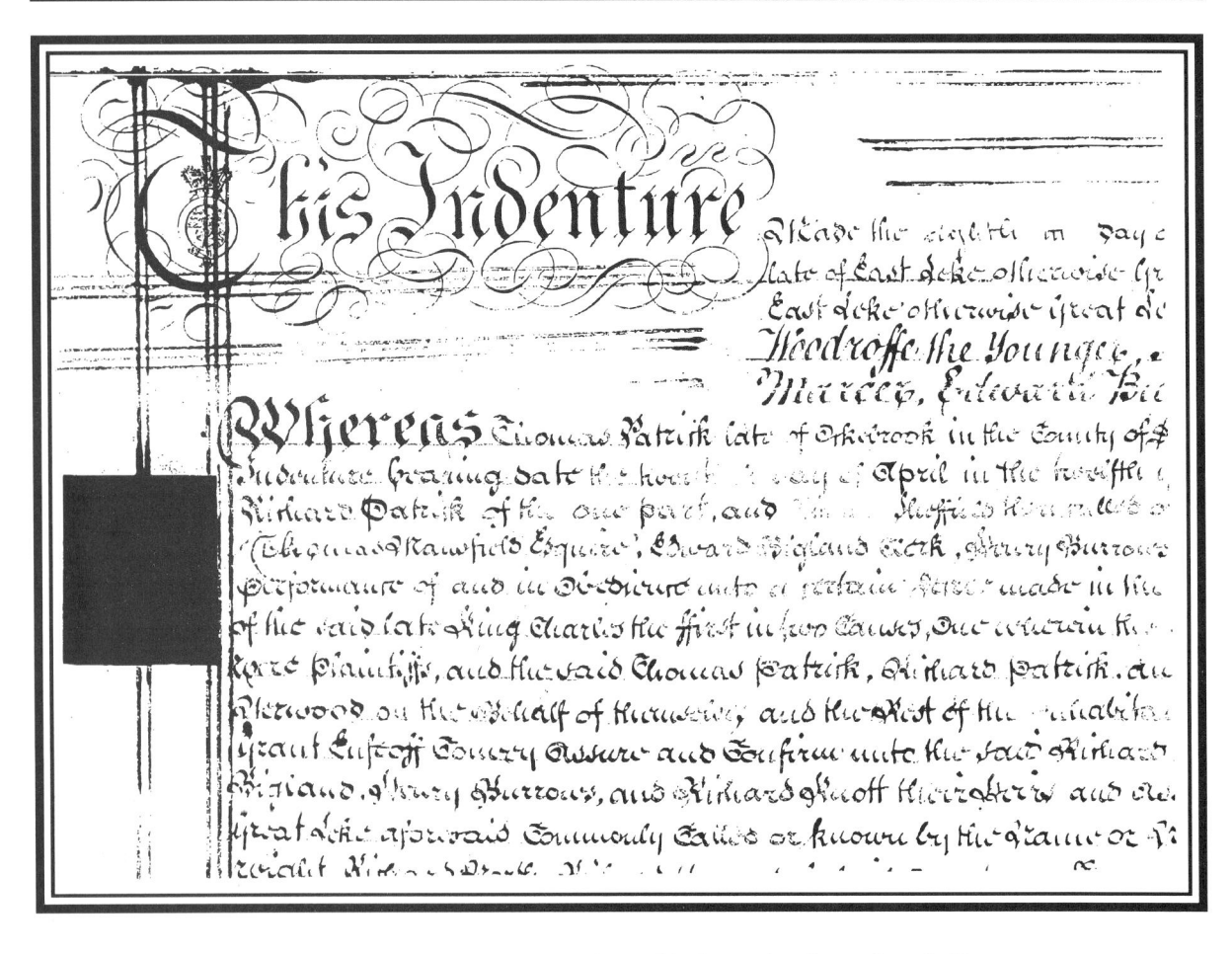

Part of the first lines of the deed establishing the Town Lands Trust

awarded to Richard Burrows for which he paid them £56 8s 0d.

The trustees in 1808 were John Angrave, Daniel Woodroffe, John Woodroffe Jnr, Thomas Angrave, Thomas Cooper Angrave, John Wootton, William Marcer, John Marcer, Edward Burrows and John Wootton Jnr. William and John Marcer were brothers and William's wife was a Burrows related to Edward Burrows, the John Woottons were father and son, T C Angrave was a nephew of Thomas Angrave whilst his brother-in-law's wife was a niece of Thomas Angrave. In 1848 William Wootton replaced John Wootton and William Burrows had been added.

In 1895 the Charity Commissioners advised the parish council that six additional trustees "may be appointed" to include a wider representation of the community. The council nominated six and the trustees in 1898 were listed in a document as the three surviving trustees in 1895 and the six council nominees – Matthew Mills, Basket Maker; Owen Smedley, Joiner; Ezra Pidcock, Grocer; Morton Handley, Licensed Victualler; Henry Smith, Miner (Gypsum) and John Smith Basket Maker. The land-owning, yeoman families of Angrave, Marcer, Woodroffe and Burrowes had died out or ceased to take an active part in village affairs. Since then vacancies through death have been filled by the trustees.

Records of lettings of the land and the disposal of the rents before 1897 have not been discovered. Since then accounts have been kept. From 25th March 1897 to 25th March 1927 the clerk to the trustees received 2½ per cent of the rents and paid the balance to the overseers for the poor – this varied annually between £12 and £25, being especially low between 1911 and 1914.

In 1897 the Great Central Railway was built through the middle of the lands, and the Trust received £566 in compensation. This was invested in Bank of England stock, yielding £6 19s 5d annually, an increase in the income.

The development of gypsum mining and a plant for the manufacture of plaster and plaster board on the adjoining land gave the trust land a potential increase in value for an extension to the buildings and railway sidings whilst the presence of gypsum beneath would provide an income from royalties if it was mined. In 1919 Mr O W Porritt, part owner of Marbleagis, the company owning the mine and plant, and Mr S Crosland, an East Leake entrepreneur, realised this and made an offer of £1550 for the Town Lands. This was approved by the Charity Commissioners but the sale did not take place. This may have been fortunate when later the British Plaster Board mined the gypsum beneath the lands and paid to the Trust a retainer and royalties.

The signatures of the original trustees of the Town Lands Trust deed

John Angrave	Thomas Cooper Angrave	John Mercer
Daniel Woodroffe	John Wootton	Edward Burrows	Thomas Angrave
John Woodroffe jnr	William Mercer	John Wootton

In 1926 the funding of the poor was transferred to the local rating system and the national social security system. The Town Land Trustees considered the situation and decided that it would be within the terms of the founding in 1637 that they could use their funds to provide services of use to the community. By 1930 there was a need for street lighting – the parish council had only limited funds for this. The trust contributed to the cost of the electricity whilst Mr O W Porritt, with his own generating plant and money, increased the number of street lamps. In 1932 - 33 the trust provided £122 7s 3d for the improvement of the Memorial Gardens and continued to meet costs of their upkeep. Since then the trust, working in co-operation with the parish council, has contributed in various ways to village activities — the village hall, sports, festivities, churchyard, Christmas carols.

JOHN BLEY circa 1674 - 1731

John Bley was a native of the Town of Leake, born about 1674 - 5 and died in London on 28th May 1731. Potter's History and publications tell us a great deal about him, probably one of the richest men of Leake. Unfortunately the church registers were defective in the middle of the seventeenth century, during the Commonwealth when the rectory became vacant, and was not filled. Consequently Potter was not able to find records of his birth and of the marriage of his parents, but he writes that John Bley was born and brought up in Joyce's manor, a house which stood to the rear of the present Brookside Farm on the west side of Brookside. William Bley owned this property about the time of John's birth. He was well off, possibly of yeoman or freeman stock, and churchwarden in 1665. The other churchwarden was George Wight. Gifts and legacies in John's will point to his daughter as John's mother. From this William Bley's son is most likely to have been his father. Maybe either or both died when John was a child and he was brought up by his grandparents. Eventually John inherited the manor, and so was Lord of the Manor.

As a young man John Bley went to London with £100, a considerable amount in those days. At that time a branch of the Wight family was established in business in London. John joined his uncle North, a brewer. Later he set up in the liquor trade and became a successful London businessman. John maintained his links with Great Leake and had inherited Joyce's manor. The house had deteriorated and he bought a plot of land on the north-west side of the High Street and built a large house in the Queen Anne style. A gable on the front half bears the initials I.B. (I is for J) and date 1715 whilst the gable on the rear half bears I.B. 1728. He transferred the name, Joyce's Manor, to his new house. Today it is a Grade II listed building, the post office, no 25 Main Street. This house was sold and at the time of the enclosures belonged to John Hollis. Later deeds suggest that the owners were Lords of Joyce's Manor but this is unlikely as the enclosure award records John Hardy as Lord of the Manor and owner of the Brookside homestead. He was a descendant of Hugh Hardy who had inherited it from John Bley.

In 1724 John Bley carried out a youthful vow to build a school in Great Leake. This school was in the Queen Anne style, similar to his house. He endowed it with £450, invested in 25 acres of land at Burton-on-the-Wolds and Wymeswold. In his will he left the schoolhouse, adjoining orchard and the endowment for the use of the school children of East Leake in trust to John Clifton, Samuel Irby and Daniel Woodroffe, trustees of the Common Meadow. It was acquired by the East Leake School Board in 1874 and continued in use for a year or two, eventually being demolished and replaced in 1877 by a new school erected to the rear.

Only the small Sheepwash Brook separated the Leake properties of Sir Thomas Parkyns, country landowner, and John Bley, London citizen, two

The Bley Endowed Free School

rich men. They were on friendly terms and Sir Thomas sent John pheasants at Christmas and placed his son in John's charge when he went to London.

John Bley's will shows that he amassed a fortune, possibly the equivalent of two to four million pounds today. The executors were Samuel Sterrop, steward of Sir Thomas Parkyns and Hugh Hardy of East Leake, a relative by marriage. He owned land and properties in Thanes Street, St Dunstan's Hill, Cross Lane, Potter Lane and Basinghall Street in London – a small fortune in themselves. As well, he had lands and properties in East Leake. He had substantial holdings in four coasting vessels and £1000 of Bank of England stock. All these were sound investments. To his kinsfolk, the Hardys, the Hopkins and the Moores, he left £2,800 worth of South Sea annuities, but it was doubtful if they had any value in view of the South Sea Bubble, a disaster which befell this enterprise.

He made monetary bequests to relations and friends amounting to £7,380. He left "To every husbandman or husbandman's widow that keeps at least one team with plows, carriages and other implements of husbandry in East Leake, £10 each, and to every cottager there, £5, except that idle family of George Doughty's". For the poor of the parishes which bordered East Leake, viz Bunny, Costock, Rempstone, Stanford, Normanton, Little Leake and Gotham he gave "£10 to each town" and for the poor of East Leake he gave £30 to be distributed by Hugh Hardy at £10 a year over three years "in the severities of winter". Also he left £50 to Hugh Hardy for the schoolmaster, Mr Richard James, being five years' salary at £10 per year. These were generous bequests as £10 was an appreciable amount in those days.

It is difficult to assess the value of £10 in the eighteenth century in today's currency. It could be the equivalent of anything between £1,000 and £10,000.

The tomb of John Bley is in the graveyard close to the east end of the church. This is a customary position for the internment of a Lord of the Manor. An outline of his will is inscribed on a slate mounted on one side (see below and p 33).

Here lyeth Interred the Body of Mr. John Bley Citizen and Distiller of LONDON Born in this Town: Whose Charity in his Lifetime and at his death was very extensive. he built the Charity School-House in this Town and by his Will gave Four hundred and fifty Pounds for the Purchase of Lands to be settled on y said School; and also Ten Pounds to each Farmer, and five Pounds to each Cottager, living here in Leake; and likewise Ten Pounds to the Poor of each Parish that border upon this Lordship, with a great many other large Legacies to his Relations, and Friends: he died in London May 28th An Dom. 1731, and was here Buried June the 3d following. In the 57th Year of his Life.

The inscription on the side of the tomb of John Bley

TRADESMEN, CRAFTSMEN AND OTHER OCCUPATIONS

From the Danish and even from the earlier English (Anglo-Saxon) settlement, most of the inhabitants of Great Leake were farmers and this continued until the weaving, lace and hosiery industries developed. It was a township and some inhabitants were tradesmen, craftsmen, a priest and retainers of the Lords of the Manors. The way of life changed with the development of a monetary economy and the availability of food, clothing and goods from world trade. The standards of living rose and in Great Leake, as throughout the country, butchers, bakers, masons, carpenters, wheelwrights, blacksmiths, drapers, cordwainers or shoemakers, tailors, victuallers, shopkeepers and grocers became a significant part of the community. They were comparatively well-off and their wills and inventories are included in the diocesan archives.

The grocers were important, providing a wide range of goods and services. They purchased goods from various sources: the local farms, regional producing areas and from the markets associated with the ports involved in world trade. Then they retailed them to the consumer in the smaller quantities which they needed. In Great Leake Enoch Watson was the grocer between the restoration of the monarchy in 1660 and his death in 1707. His will has not been traced but the inventory of his goods reveals the activities of a grocer and the ways of life in the period of prosperity following the puritan austerity of the earlier seventeenth century. The yeomen and other better-off families had more leisure and a social life in which to enjoy richer foods and drinks, luxury clothes, fine furnishing and tableware.

The total value of the inventory was £80. This indicates that it was a large business. A satisfactory method of assessing the value of the medieval pound sterling in today's terms has not been evolved but even at a modest thousand times, this would make the business worth over £80,000 in today's money. The value of his house, properties and land is not known

Enoch Watson was selling a wide range of goods in Great Leake and the neighbouring villages. Diets had been enriched and he sold sugar, currants, raisins, treacle, ginger and pepper, mainly imported foods. As ale was widely used he stocked ground corn or malt for brewing. Smoking and drinking had spread as part of the social change and he sold wine and spirits (recorded as "strong water") as well as tobacco and snuff (tobacco dust).

Fine materials, many imported from Holland, were stocked to provide social (non-working) clothes for men and women. Listed in the inventory were silk, linen, tansy, worsted, damask (a rich patterned fabric) and figured materials of wool, linen or cotton. He stocked furnishing fabrics, dimity (striped or checked cotton cloth woven for beds and hangings), ticking (a striped material for bolsters and mattresses) and canvas made of flax or hemp. These could be made up by the womenfolk, dressmakers and tailors for whom buttons, threads, hooks and eyes, pins, ribbon, tape and buckram were available at his shop.

He stocked sundry household goods – brooms, candles, soap, wash balls (used for washing hands or face). People corresponded and he provided the writing paper and materials for making ink, lac (a red, resinous dye) and copperas (green, white and blue dyes). Medical care was mostly through common knowledge and medicines were supplied from a nest of boxes, a chest of small drawers.

The inventory lists the tools of his trade – weights and scales, together with tubs, barrels, casks and coffers for dry and liquid storage.

In effect he was operating a general store, requiring finance and contacts at a distance from Great Leake. Included in the inventory was £30, suggesting that he was acting as a banker, even advancing monies for business and personal needs. Some grocers were the founders of today's banks.

Watson's house is described in the inventory as consisting of the main room, a kitchen and two bedchambers. There was a fireplace – this dates the house at not much earlier than 1600 and similar to those of the yeomen of his time. It was well furnished. There were flock beds, curtains and valances and he had pewter dishes, all signs of affluence. He had two cows, swine and crops of corn, peas and hay indicating that he had rights in the common fields. Enoch Watson was prosperous.

THE CHURCH OF LEAKE — THE ECCLESIASTICAL BODY

In 1206 the Church of Leke was held in two equal parts and in 1207 William de Leke was the first rector, appointed by the Prior and Convent of Repton. In 1347 the two moieties were disputed but only one rector was appointed, Robert de Clypston. The church continued as a single benefice with one rector until 1882.

In 1306 Sir Henry Sutton is described as Rector of St Leonard's of Leke and in 1317 Cardinal Raymond de Fargis as Parson of Great Lek. Roger Smyth, rector 1462 to 1473, desired to be buried before the altar in St Helena, West Leake. From this time the rectors based themselves in West Leake and St Helena was called the Mother Church until the division of the benefice in 1882.

Upon the dissolution of Calke priory in 1537 the advowson passed to Sir John Porte. His daughter married George Hastings who acquired the patronage in 1567, and for most of the time thereafter it was held by members of the Hastings family.

The rector was responsible for the maintenance of services in both East and West Leake, appointing curates to assist him. According to Potter, curates were appointed in 1298, 1300, 1553, 1626 and 1646. Edward Tomson was appointed between 1646 and 1697 and thereafter curates were appointed regularly until 1882.

In 1981 the churches of East Leake, West Leake, Costock, Rempstone and Stanford-on-Soar, together with Holy Cross Convent at Rempstone were formed into a united benefice with a rector, assistant priest, honorary priests and readers to provide the services and needs of all.

ST LEONARD'S AND ST MARY'S CHURCH AT GREAT LEAKE

The minster church at Great Leake was dedicated to St Leonard. Much of the original eleventh century Saxon church has been identified within the present church of St Mary's. The north wall of the nave, with its Saxon north door, is virtually complete. The east and west ends of the south wall can be seen, whilst the pillars of the south arcade are standing on the foundations of the south wall. The two lower stages of the tower remain, with the entrance from the nave to the priest's chamber in the upper stage. During the restoration of the church in 1886 the foundations of the Saxon chancel were found and their size recorded. It is believed that there was a south aisle and a door opposite the north door. From this information Owen Wood and David Clarke have drawn a representation of the Saxon church (p 3).

Early in the twelfth century the church was reconstructed by Harold of Leke and his son Alan. The south aisle was built in the Early English style with an arcade of four arches, matching arches were cut into the east and west end of the nave, and the roof was raised by about two feet. The chancel was extended and some changes were made to the tower. The twelfth century font has been removed recently from beneath the westernmost arch of the south aisle.

Cardinal de Fargis was Rector from 1308 to 1347. He was a wealthy man and a pluralist holding several offices in the church. He extended the chancel, fitting it with fine windows in the decorated style. At the same time the traceries of the windows in the south aisle were replaced to match the windows of the chancel. De Fergis replaced the Lady Chapel at the east end of the south aisle with a chantry. On the completion of these works the dedication of the church was changed to St Mary, a popular dedication at that time. Following its collapse, the chancel was rebuilt in 1884 - 86 and the east window was carefully rebuilt in the original style.

Changing liturgies and fashions in the fifteenth century resulted in changes to the church without much disturbance to the fourteenth century building. To provide more light a clerestory was added to the nave and a flat leaded roof replaced the high pitched thatched roof of the chancel and nave. The uppermost stage of the tower was rebuilt and a parapet and spire were added. The extra weight required a substantial buttress on the north

Thirteenth to Eighteenth Centuries

east corner of the tower and buttresses on the north wall of the nave and the outside wall of the south aisle. A vestry was built about the north door of the nave. The nave with a rammed earth floor was an open space. Three fifteenth century poppy head benches and five seventeenth century benches have survived from this period.

Following the Reformation during the reign of Henry VIII, the church was despoiled. The chantry built by Cardinal de Fargis was removed, together with any tombs and monuments. Fortunately three "willed, December 3rd 1346, that his body should be buried in the Church". The Umfreys were an important family in the area at this time.

The stone altars were removed by order of Elizabeth I and replaced by wooden tables. One in the chantry survives, despite having been thrown out during the 1886 restoration but recovered from a garden, cleaned and put back.

The church suffered from neglect and the north wall of the chancel collapsed in 1836. In 1845 the interior underwent major alterations – the chancel

LEAKE			
1207	Robert de Leke	1598	Thurston Chapleyn
1228	Henry de Gray	1612	John Davenant
1239	John le Vavasour	1620	Edward Bigland
1243	Walter le Vavasour	1662	John Moore
1250	Henry le Vavasour	1667	John Davys
1281	Roger de Hengham	1717	Michael Stanhope
1298	Henry de Sutton on Sore	1737	Granville Wheler
1308	Raymond William de Fargis	1770	Robert Hemington
1347	Robert de Clypston	1772	Edward Ellis
1364	Thomas de Bildeston	1795	Theophilus Henry Hastings
1387	Roger de Pickeryng	1804	George Holcombe
1404	John de Barford	1836	John Bateman
1441	John Toralde		
1458	Richard Mysin	EAST LEAKE	
1462	Roger Smyth	1882	Casper Lewis Vashon Baker
1473	William Fitzherbert	1888	Sidney Pell Potter
1476	Nicholas Fitzherbert	1918	Thomas Cooper Angrave
1517	Julian Crosby	1931	Robert Cecil Smith
1554	Richard Walker	1952	Harold Arthur Kirton
1567	Matthew Hutton	1963	Fredrick John Legge
	(later Archbishop of York)	1977	David Walter Skyrme James
		1984	Stephen John Smith
1568	Thomas Baldwyn	1997	Vacant

Rectors of Leake and East Leake

pieces were placed outside the south door of the church and reputedly mark the graves of four soldiers killed in a skirmish during the Civil War (1664). Recent examination of these has identified them as a damaged coffin lid and two parts of a monument. The coffin could have been that of a rector; the monument that of a Leake or a prominent inhabitant such as William Umfrey who screen and the manor pew were removed and high box pews erected in the nave.

At some time a gallery had been erected at the west end of the nave but this was removed in 1860. It is likely that the choir with orchestral accompaniment occupied this gallery. The shawm, a vamping horn, hangs in the south aisle. John Savage played this in the church choir during the curacy of Rev James Boultbee 1854 - 1858. Vamping horns were invented in 1670 by Sir Samuel Morland for use both at sea and on land and as megaphones; they could be heard clearly over one mile. They were adapted for use by church choirs. The East Leake shawm is one of eight remaining in this country. It is light to carry, being made of tin with a mouthpiece and a bell with a diameter of 21½ inches (546 mm). The sliding tube enables it to be extended from 4 ft 1 in to 7 ft 9 in (1.24 m to 2.36 m).

A clock by Richard Roe of Epperston was installed in the tower in 1683. Roe had been producing clocks for most of the seventeenth century and this is an improved version with a pendulum and anchor escapement. It struck the half hours, but had no face. Massive stone weights provided the power, and daily winding was necessary. In 1794 the parish clerk was paid £1 per annum for this. It fell into decay in the late nineteenth century and was restored in 1991. It is in working order and has been put at the foot of the tower. It was replaced by a clock installed by public subscription to commemorate the coronation of King George V on June 22nd 1911. This was a mechanical clock with faces on the south and east walls of the tower. The movement lasted until 1985 and was replaced early in 1987 by an electronic clock controlled by signals from a master clock at Rugby.

A complete restoration of the church took place in 1884 - 86. The rector, Rev Baker, had trained as an architect and brought in Mr W S Weatherby, who had trained with him under Sir Gilbert Scott, architect for Liverpool Cathedral. They decided to restore the church to its sixteenth century appearance. The chancel was rebuilt upon the former foundations using the old materials and copies of surviving parts of the original tracery of the east window. In place of the north wall and a brick vestry, a vestry and organ chamber was built in stone. The nave was refurbished and the high box pews cut down to the present ones. Later an unsightly brick south porch was rebuilt and both lectern and pulpit restyled in 1902. An outside door to the south porch and a screen to the ringers' chamber at the base of the tower are recent improvements which have enhanced the beauty of the church so carefully restored to its sixteenth century appearance.

Fifteenth century poppy seat and two seventeenth century seats in the church

NON-CONFORMITY

In Elizabethan times the gentry, gentlemen and tradespeople of towns and open villages such as Great Leake had been liberated from ecclesiastical and feudal control. They disliked the restrictive practices, such as compulsory church attendance, imposed by the Anglican Church and were responsible for the setting up of the religious sects, Baptists, Quakers, Unitarians and Methodists. In 1604, four people in Great Leake refused to sign the affirmation of their support for the Anglican Church, but all the inhabitants over sixteen took the Protestation in March 1641/42; none refused.

In 1669 there were four Anabaptists in Great Leake and there was a Baptist Convention in Rempstone attended by some two hundred people from the surrounding villages. During the early part of the eighteenth century the new General Baptist movement spread in Nottinghamshire. At Great Leake there was one of the four main centres. This was a large and vigorous community and from 1802 to 1881 included the villages around Great Leake and Wymeswold. In 1757 Thomas Clarke, a lace and hosier merchant, gave land for the chapel and graveyard at the east end of Main Street. He lent £100 to meet the cost of the building and this was soon refunded. The east and north walls of this chapel can be seen in the present chapel. In the early years baptisms took place in the nearby brook, a crowd of three thousand being present at the baptism of 24 persons in 1836.

A Sunday School was started in George Burrows's cottage in 1807 and this was followed by the building of a vestry for the use of the school and in 1809 by chambers for the minister. At the same time it was necessary to appoint trustees to replace those appointed in 1756.

In 1836 the increase in the congregation required a larger chapel, achieved by extending the 1757 building to include a gallery and baptism pool. In 1977 the vestry was extended and up-to-date facilities installed.

In the eighteenth century Methodism developed and owes much to the missionary travels of John Wesley and the evangelical contribution of his hymn-writing brother Charles. John was active in the Leicester and Nottingham areas in 1741 - 42 and in 1772, received support from Selina Countess of Huntington. In 1772 John Wesley was at the Hoton home of John and Elizabeth Angrave, one of an East Leake yeoman family. Such meetings resulted in the formation of Christian societies organised by the lay members. In 1798 John Angrave gave a plot of land in the centre of East Leake for a chapel, the Wesleyan Methodist Church. It was extended in 1827 by 8 feet (2.4 m) to include a gallery. Today the date stone is in the boundary wall of the Village Hall. In 1863 a new Victorian style chapel was built on the opposite side of the main street and the original chapel became the schoolroom. In 1933 a schoolroom was added to the rear of the Victorian chapel and the old schoolroom was sold to become part of the village hall. Fifty years on both of the earlier chapels were demolished and a multi-purpose building erected at the rear of the nineteenth century chapel, the main hall serving as church, schoolroom and general meeting room for social and business meetings. It was opened on 17th April 1983.

Late in the eighteenth century, in the tradition of the early Methodists, an evangelistic movement arose within Methodism and in 1811 the Primitive Methodist Church was formed. The first meeting in Nottingham took place on Christmas Eve 1815. In 1819, at a conference held in Nottingham, John Garner, a young man from East Leake, resolved that the movement needed a guiding hand, took a ladder and painted CANAAN STREET in large letters on the building – the choir had just sung 'Canaan, bright Canaan, I'm bound for the land of Canaan'.

John and his two brothers became members and took a leading part in the Primitive Methodist Church. They were the sons of a framework knitter who came from Kegworth to East Leake in 1804. Their father died whilst they were still young. Their mother, Elizabeth, was an earnest and constant member of the Wesleyan Methodist Church for many years.

The eldest son was the Rev John Garner (1800 - 1856). He was General Missionary Secretary, and spent most of his life organising several districts throughout the country. Between the years 1843 and 1854 he was six times president of the annual conference.

The second son, the Rev William Garner (1802 - 1881) began his ministry in 1822, preaching at his mother's house. He drafted the church's legislation and administered denominational laws. He served in many offices throughout the country. He was President of the Annual Conference in 1859 and 1861.

The third son, the Rev James Garner (born at East Leake 1809, died 1895) began his ministry in 1830 and was active in the development of the church throughout the country and in various offices. He wrote several books on the history and theology of Primitive Methodism. He was President of the Annual Conference in 1864 and 1871.

Elizabeth and these three sons are commemorated on a tablet in the entrance hall to the Methodist Church. The Rev John Kemp Garner (1853 - 1915), son of Rev John Garner, emigrated to Canada and played a leading role in the formation of the Canadian church.

For about one hundred years the Great Leake Primitive Methodists met in a small chapel at the rear of 1 Costock Road. It had 67 seats. The pew rents were £16 17s 0d from 22 members in 1881, and had declined to 8s 0d in 1910.

The Anglican Church was against the growth of non-conformity and opposed it by word and deed. In Great Leake the Rev Theophilus Henry Hastings, curate from 1755 to 1763 and rector from 1795 to 1804, spoke and wrote strongly against the Methodists, Jacobins and Atheists. During his curacy, the Baptist Church was being built, and during his time as rector the Methodists built their first church. In 1800 he published 'Eight Sermons upon the 16th Chap of the Revelation of St John, preached in the consolidated churches of West and East Leake'. This did not seem to have created ill feeling within the village, a community led by yeomen, many of whom were active members of the Methodist and Baptist groups. Even a hundred years later the rector, Rev S P Potter, was actively opposed to the Baptists and Methodists. The ill-feeling between him and two elders of the Methodist Church, Thomas Needham father and son, is recalled to this day. In his history of East Leake, Potter devotes several pages to the Rev Hastings and his sermons, but gives little information about the activities of the Methodists and Baptists and the sole reference to the building of their churches is in a footnote recording that of the Baptist Church in 1757.

A family situation is another aspect of the attitude of the Rev Hastings to the issues between the established Church and non-conformity. The Hastings family had been patrons of the Leake rectory since 1567 when the patronage came to George Hastings (p 21). In 1737 the Rev Granville Wheeler became Rector of Leake. His wife was a daughter of Theophilus Hastings, 9th Earl of Huntington and they cared for their kinsman, Theophilus Henry Hastings who became Rev Wheeler's curate in 1755. Selina Countess of Huntington, wife of the 9th Earl was interested in the evangelical movement of the non-conformists and was notable for the formation of the Countess of Huntington Connexion which advanced her views. In his biography of the Huntington Peerage, Nugent Bell writes that Theophilus Hastings incurred the severe displeasure of the Dowager Countess Selina through his zealous support of the established faith and animated opposition to Methodists. It is likely that he felt that her support of the non-conformists reduced the material benefits he might have expected from her. His relations with the family were also strained by his claim to the peerage which went to the Earl of Moira upon the death of the 10th Earl.

PART FOUR — FARMING AND ENCLOSURE

Early enclosure — the Act of 1798 for the enclosure of Great Leake, the public and private roads and footways, main awards of land and farming in the nineteenth and twentieth centuries

ENCLOSURE

The system of open fields and common lands continued throughout the medieval period. In Great Leake from time to time freemen and yeomen were able to consolidate their strips in the open fields and to enclose both these areas and grazing land adjacent to the farmsteads. The conditions for this varied from place to place – thus some villages became extensive grazings for sheep. By the end of the seventeenth century there were advances in knowledge. New ideas about crops and the management of arable land were associated with advances in livestock feeding and breeding. Only a few miles from Great Leake, Robert Bakewell at Dishley was one of the pioneers in the improvement of cattle and sheep. The restrictions imposed by the fixed cropping of the open fields prevented the growing of root crops such as turnips and mangold wurzels and the common grazing of cattle and sheep did not give the individual farmer control over the use of the improved sires which were available from such breeders as Bakewell.

Enclosures took place by mutual agreement encouraged by enlightened landowners and farmers. Such enclosures obtained confirmation from the Court of Chancery and later by Private Act of Parliament. By the end of the eighteenth century enclosure was increasing rapidly. About 1790 the yeomen of Great Leake were considering enclosure and in 1798 an Act of Parliament was passed for dividing and inclosing (sic) the fields, closes, meadows, common pastures and wastes. This was carried out by the commissioners Edward Dawson of Donington Park, John Boultbee of Bunny, John Seagrave of Kirkby Bellars, John Chamberlain of Cropredy (Oxford) and John Bailey of Nottingham. John Bailey was appointed to survey the land and prepare a plan of the enclosures. The award and plan were published in the year 1799 (Plan p 27).

The first part of the award set out the public and private roads, public and private bridle roads, footways and paths, with detailed instructions as to their construction and maintenance. The commissioners had powers to close ancient roads and ways and to appoint a surveyor or surveyors of the highways for the maintenance of the public roads. Two plots of land were awarded for the supply of sand and gravel.

The road from Coleorton via Hathern to Rempstone was a turnpike and was not to be changed. Public roads 40 feet (12 metres) wide for carriages and for livestock were built or redefined mainly to the neighbouring villages – Little Leke, Normanton (part of former Millgate Way), Rempstone and Kegworth, including Kirk Ley Road, Gotham, Bunny and Thrumpton. Likewise public roads, 12 feet (3.6 metres) wide for riding and pack horses and for livestock, were defined – one from Bunny and Gotham, and another from Little Leke to Rempstone (the neolithic Streetway). Footways and private roads were also set out.

Thus the plan of the village was set and was the basis for the expansion in housing in the next two hundred years. Since then one or two roads and footpaths have been closed or diverted.

The second part of the award defines the plots awarded to 55 owners in consideration of their entitlement to land from the fields, commons and wastes.

Thus the Rector and his successors were awarded parts of the open fields, lammas closes[4], meadows, pastures and common and waste ground to equal in value the Glebe land and Common Right belonging to the rectors together with such parcels

---

4. Lammas closes were common fields, mown for hay and opened for grazing on the first of August.

FARMING AND ENCLOSURE

Computer scanned and regenerated

Plan of the
PARISH of

GREAT LEAKE

in the county of
NOTTINGHAMSHIRE

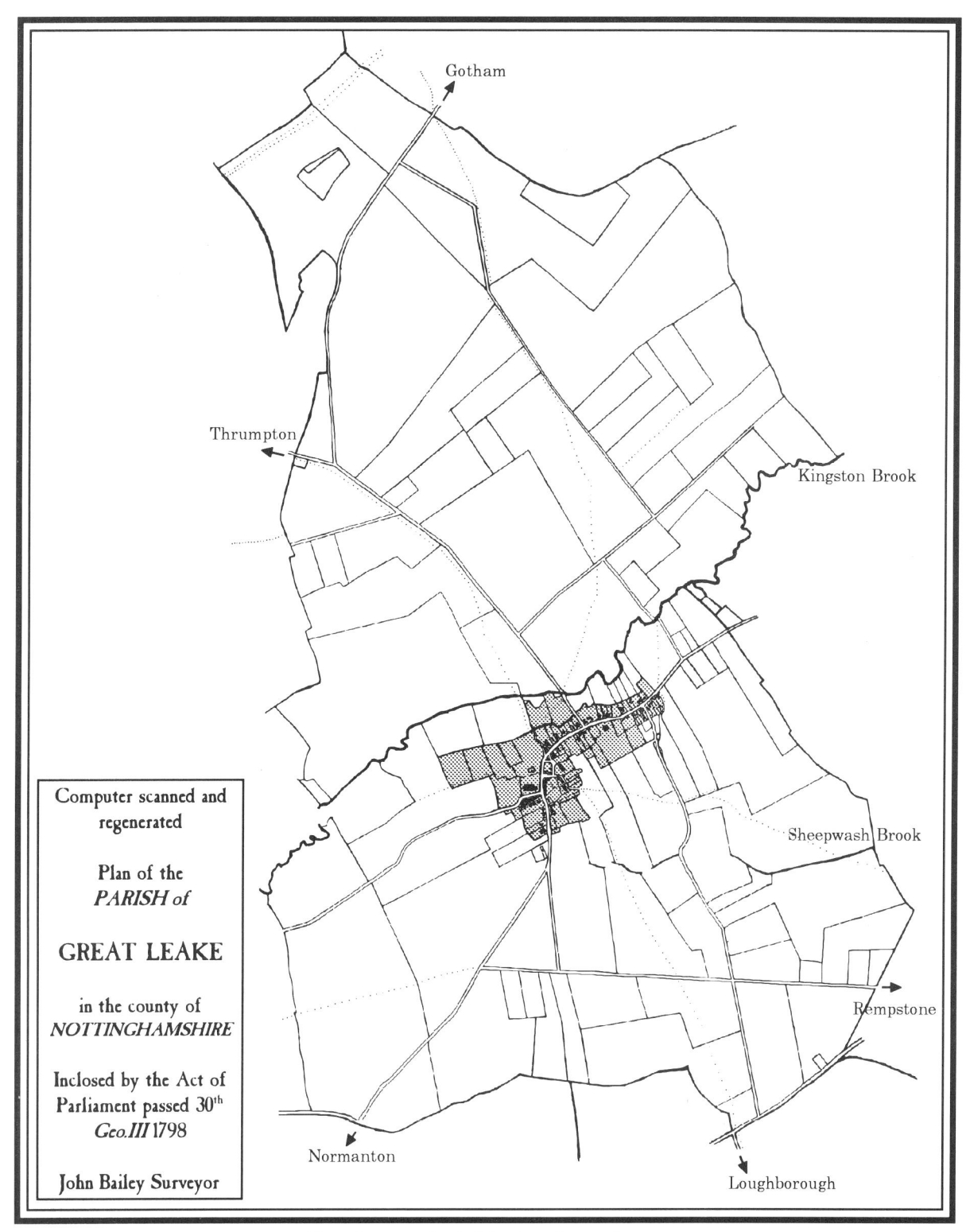

Inclosed by the Act of
Parliament passed 30th
Geo.III 1798

John Bailey Surveyor

Map showing the fields after the enclosure
(For clarity a number of details have been omitted)
The map has been scanned from a photograph of the original enclosure map in the County Archives

PAGE TWENTY SEVEN

FARMING AND ENCLOSURE

as would be equal in value to one full seventh part of all the land to be divided and enclosed and also of other yards, garden, orchards, homestead and enclosed lands subject to tithe in lieu of and full satisfaction for all manner of tithes of corn, grain, hay, wool and lamb and all other great and small dues. For this the Rector received 416 acres 3 roods 29 poles for tithes and had the glebe 48 acres 2 roods 3 poles – a total holding of 465 acres 2 roods 29 poles. This land was tenanted by Wm Angrave and Wm Kirk.

There were three manors and the Lords received plots for their rights and interests at an average of ten acres for the average value of their interest. Thus Sir Thomas Parkyns of Bunny was allotted 17 acres 2 roods 29 poles in respect of the Manors of Shirley and Cosby. This included a water house and spring supplying water to his Bunny property. In all, he was allotted 422 acres 0 roods 28 poles for his several rights. This land was farmed by tenants including William Angrave. John Hardy was allotted 192 acres 2 roods 9 poles including 6 acres

Owner	Area awarded Acres	Owner	Area awarded Acres
Rev Henry Hastings	416	Charles Vere-Dashwood	4
Sir Thomas Parkyns	422	Thomas Dexter	2
John Hardy	192	Loughborough Charities	16
John Hollis	163	Richard Goodacre	35 perches
Thomas Hall	124	Samuel Grundy	4
Mary Aldridge	51	William Harrison	3
Hannah Alsebruck	1	William Marcer	31
John Angrave	47	John Marcer	22
William Angrave	9	Rt Hon Lord Middleton	1
Thomas Angrave	46	William Miller	1 rood
Francis Asher	8	Thomas Miller	2
Elizabeth Attenborrow	39	John Morris	3
Trustees for Baptist Society	33 perches	William and Nathaniel Neal	26
William Blount	3	Richard Norman	2
Thomas Bosworth	1 rood	Joseph Oldershaw	19
Benjamin Broomhead	24 perches	William Plowright	16
Trustees for Bunny Poor	3	Samuel Rowbotham	1
Richard Burton	1 rood	Thomas Smith	1
Edward Burrows	52	John Smith	7
Richard Burrows	97	Matthew Steel	12
John and Robert Clarke	9	George Thompson	49
Jane Clarke	1	Joseph Towle	81
John Cragg	30	Trustees for Great Leke Town	21
Jarvis Cragg	4	William Gregory Williams	2
George Augustus Curzon	0	John Wootton	81
Charles Cross	6	Daniel Woodroffe	145
Joseph Cross	6	John Woodroffe	4

Enclosure Award 1799 — Area awarded to each owner of land

PAGE TWENTY EIGHT

Size group	Number of owners	Area awarded			
		Acres	Roods	Poles	
100 - 466 acres	6	1514	0	12	
50 - 100 acres	5	362	3	20	64.0
30 - 50 acres	6	245	0	32	15.4
10 - 30 acres	9	149	1	5	10.4
3 - 10 acres	13	76	0	7	6.3
1 - 3 acres	13	16	0	21	3.2
Under 1 acre	3	0	2	12	0.7
TOTAL	55	2364	0	29	

Land to supply sand and gravel for roads — 3 Acres 0 Roods 30 Poles

Enclosure Award 1799 — Distribution of land by size of holding

1 rood 24 poles as Lord of Joyce's Manor. Together these three owners received 1140 acres 1 rood 16 poles — almost half of the total area enclosed.

John Hollis was awarded 163 acres 0 roods 14 poles and Thomas Hall, a Nottingham butcher likewise 124 acres 3 roods 7 poles. These two men were not farmers in East Leake and let these lands to tenants — thus William Angrave was tenant of most of John Hollis's land.

Most of the other enclosed land was awarded to the descendants of the yeomen — some still farming their lands. The principal yeomen to receive land (the acreage received in brackets) were Daniel Woodroffe (146 acres), the cousins Richard Burrows (97 acres) and Edward Burrows (52 acres), John Wootton (81 acres), the Angraves John and Thomas (47 acres each), and the Marcers – William (32 acres) and John (22 acres). Two plots were awarded to charities, 21 acres to the Town lands Trust and 16 acres for certain charities in Loughborough.

Overall 89.8 per cent of the enclosed land went to 17 owners with 30 acres or more. A further 6.3 per cent was held by nine owners, all of whom were either farming or rented the land for farming.

This leaves 29 owners with less than ten acres. These plots were a few acres attached to homesteads of elderly relatives of farmers, of workers associated with farming and of persons whose primary occupation was in professions or trades.

The enclosure award describes the village as it was at the end of the eighteenth century with 118 houses and a population of 608 persons.

Enclosure was expensive. The landowners paid the fees for the Inclosure Act, the commissioners for their work and expenses and John Bailey for the survey of the parish and the plan of the enclosures. The parish was responsible for the new public roads and bridle ways and the vestry levied rates to meet these costs. The principal rate payers were the landowners and farmers. The owners were required to fence and hedge the plots and to set out and maintain the private roads and footpaths.

Farming had experienced a period of prosperity during the latter half of the eighteenth century and the Napoleonic Wars. The landowners were receiving higher rents and the farmers increased profits, and farming was able to meet these costs of enclosure. Some of the owners of the smaller plots may have had difficulties in finding the money, but there is no evidence of general hardship or loss of the land.

FARMING — NINETEENTH AND TWENTIETH CENTURIES

Enclosure was followed by a considerable investment in farmsteads. In 1798 - 99 the rector built a substantial farmstead for the tenant of part of the land awarded to the rector for tithes. This was on glebe land to the south of the green and consisted of a three-storey farmhouse, an attached cottage, barns, cattle sheds and a farmyard. Soon after this ten farmsteads were built upon farms which had been set out away from the main street and green. In 1835, Brook Furlong Farm was built on the Kingston Brook by the Costock border. Since then only two farmsteads have been built. In 1877 G H Angrave, a Leicester hosier and one of the Angraves who had farmed and owned land in the village for two or three hundred years, built the Poplars, later called Hall, on the road to West Leake. This was a large Victorian establishment with servants quarters, kitchens, laundry, stables for horses and carriages, barns and a gardener's cottage. In 1892 Richard Ratcliffe, a Leicester brewer, built a farmstead as a Home Farm for the Stanford Hall estate. This farm included land which was under the jurisdiction of Stanford at the time of Domesday, 1086.

The farmers in the village extended their houses and built barns and housing for livestock. Some of these can be identified by the incorporation of their initials and the date in the brickwork. By now, brick had become the principal building material – in some cases first floors and extensions were added to the original timber-framed buildings, whilst in other cases brick houses were built on the original foundations.

The middle of the nineteenth century was known as the Golden Age of farming. In 1851 there were 20 farmers employing 79 workers, in all 99 people plus women and children at busy times involved in farming. Including young and old members of their families, about one-fifth of the population, that is 50 out of 250 households, relied upon farming.

During the 1860s and 1870s William Braithwaite was farming at Welldales. This was one of the larger farms in East Leake. He rented more land in nearby Kingston. The farm was mainly grassland on which he kept cows, cattle and sheep. The milk was made into butter and sold locally. He grew about 60 acres of wheat, barley and beans for sale and for feed to his livestock. In 1871 he was employing three men and three boys. Some of his men were hired at the annual fairs held in East Leake. Five horses were kept for haulage and the farm operations, ploughing, cultivation, haymaking and harvesting.

Another farmer made butter, cheese and bacon from his farm, and sold these in his grocery store on Brookside.

The land-owning and farming families of the later medieval period were dying out during the nineteenth century. The Parkyns of Bunny and the Hardys of East Leake – leading landowners at the enclosure – had disposed of most of their lands by the middle of the century. Gradually the families of the medieval yeomen, the Angraves, Marcers, Norths, Woodroffes and Woottons, had died out or were farming much less land by the end of the century. The Oldershaws and Burrowes faded out in the twentieth century and by 1940 only one of the farming families at the time of the enclosure were still farming in East Leake – the Kirks.

During the last 25 years of the nineteenth century there was an increase in the number of cow-keepers in East Leake. This was the result of a combination of circumstances both national and local. The national population was rising and there were changes in the standards of living. Dairy products, particularly butter and cheese, became part of the diet of the lower classes and were cheaper. People were also drinking tea and coffee and using more milk in cooking, which required a daily delivery by retail milk rounds. Milk was now replacing ale. At the same time there was a national depression, resulting in a fall in the prices of farm products – cattle, sheep and particularly corn. Farmers in this area of the Midlands were able to adapt to these changes – they had experience in butter and cheese making and could increase the number of cows kept, partly by changing from rearing cattle and sheep for meat, partly by using their home-grown corn to feed them instead of selling it and partly by changing arable land to grassland. Milking cows required more farm workers and this counter-balanced the reduction

THE OPEN FIELDS

COMMON LAND AND MEADOWS

HILL FIELD

BRICKLIFFE FIELD

WOODGATE FIELD

Computer generated map showing the

Open Fields

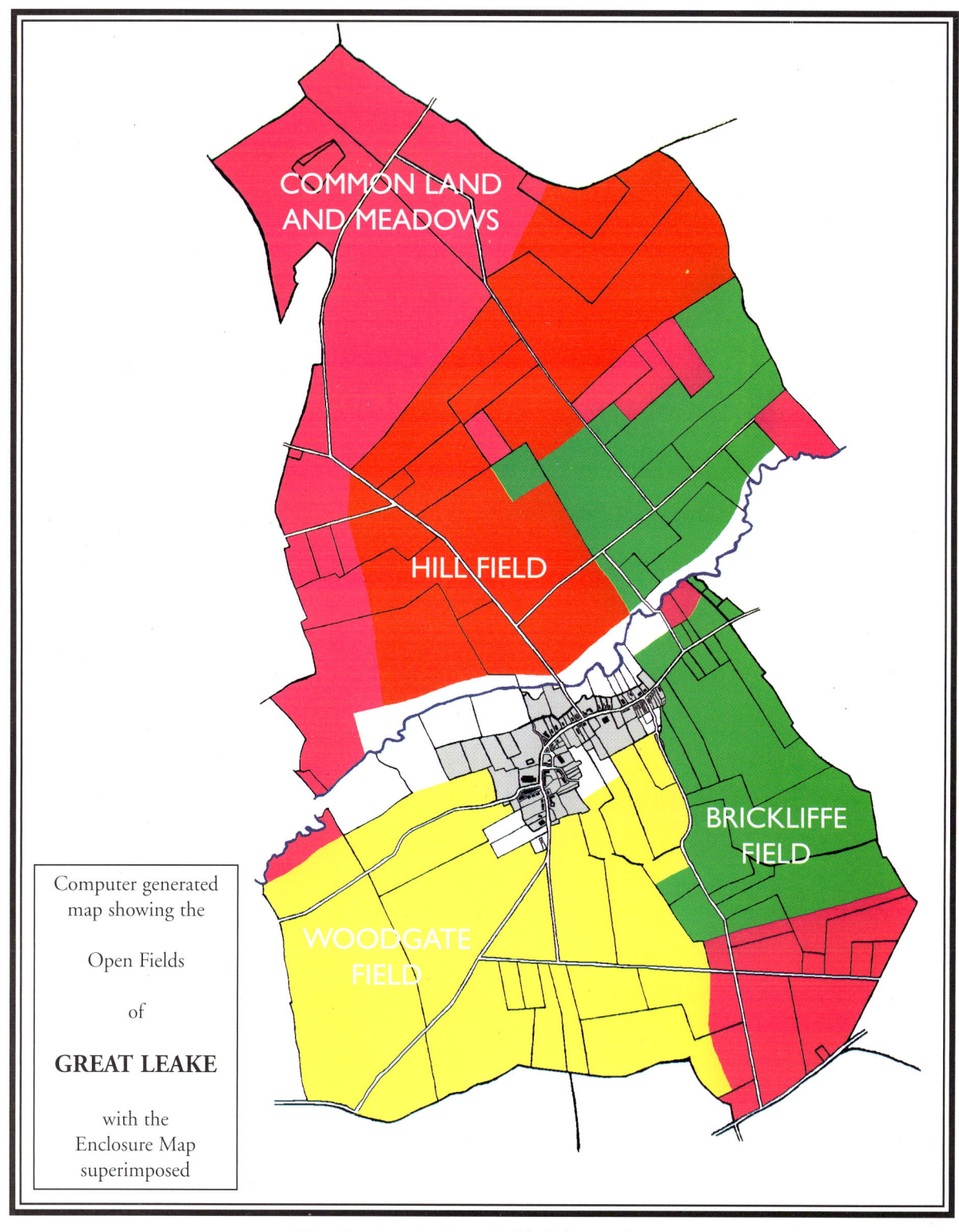

of

GREAT LEAKE

with the Enclosure Map superimposed

Map showing the Open Fields before enclosure
(For clarity a number of details have been omitted)

PAGE THIRTY ONE

ST MARY'S CHURCH

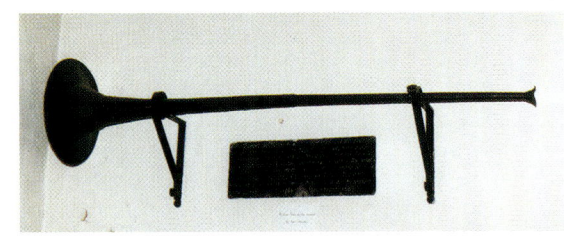

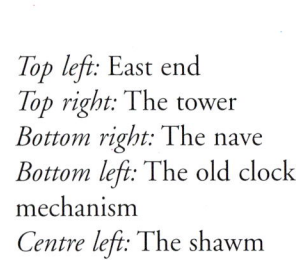

Top left: East end
Top right: The tower
Bottom right: The nave
Bottom left: The old clock mechanism
Centre left: The shawm

PAGE THIRTY TWO

Top left: John Bley's tomb in the churchyard
Top right: The first Joyce's manor – now Brookside farm
Centre right: The second Joyce's manor – now the post office
Bottom right: The present Brookside School, formerly the junior school – successor to John Bley's school and close to where it originally stood

Old Houses

Top left: Shirley's manor – now old Hall Farm, next to the church
Centre left and right: A former yeoman's house oposite the church
Bottom left: A selection of old cottages in the Nook
Bottom right: Timber framed cottage in the nook – one of only a small number left in the village

MAIN STREET

Top left: The War Memorial
Top right: Main Street – looking east from near the post office
Centre left: The new Methodist church
Centre right: The village hall – showing the original hall and the more recent extension
Bottom left: The pinfold
Bottom right: The Baptist chapel

PAGE THIRTY FIVE

GREAT CENTRAL RAILWAY

Top: East Leake station in 1970 shortly before demolition
Centre: British Railways 9F 2-10-0 no 92089 arrives with the 6.15 pm Hucknall Central to Leicester Central, an excursion train returning from an air display at Hucknall
Bottom: Royal Scot 4-6-0 no 46123 "3rd Carabinier" on 23rd June 1962 with the 12.15 pm Saturdays only Ramsgate to Derby Friargate express

BRITISH GYPSUM LIMITED

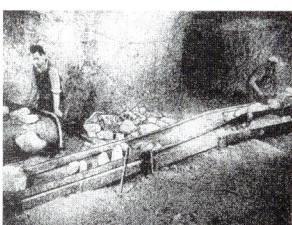

Top: A recent aerial view if the British Gypsum factory at East Leake
Bottom left: Plasterboard manufacturing lines
Bottom right: An early picture showing gypsum rock being conveyed to the surface

Parish Council

The Parish Council 1995

Back row (left to right): Graham Jones (Clerk), Tom Gwynne, Melvyn Gwynne, Richard Jenks, Vivienne Thurman, John Cursham, Bryan Davis, Ron Hetherington, Mollie Jaques and Albert England (Deputy Clerk)
Front row: Lynn Davis, Marie Males, John Needham (Chairman), Avril Bagshaw (Vice Chairman), Sonia Burton and Frank Godber *Absent:* Mike Bagshaw

The Parish Council 1999

Back row (left to right): Peter Warren, Jan Palmer, Jim Brown (Litter Warden), Keith Hodgkinson, Peter Temple, Amanda Gallagher, Trevor Palmer, Vivienne Thurman, Paul Jaques, Marie Males and Wyn Sheppard
Front row: Sue Lewis (Administrative Assistant), Hilary Morrissey, Chris Robinson, Mollie Jaques (Chariman), Paul Morrissey (Vice Chairman) and Graham Jones (Clerk)

caused by mechanisation. Milk did not keep fresh for more than a day and a daily delivery to every household was necessary. Retail milk rounds were formed by some of the East Leake milk producers to supply the population of the village and nearby Loughborough, both of which were growing. Overall this meant some change in the appearance of East Leake, but not in the numbers of people employed. The village did not suffer from the effect of low corn prices as did the arable areas of England.

The Board of Agriculture, newly formed in 1889, fostered farming education and an officer was appointed in Nottinghamshire in 1891. He arranged classes in farmhouse butter and cheese making in East Leake. Soon he became Director of Studies in Agriculture at Nottingham University College and addressed a meeting of farmers in East Leake. He and Lord Belper were the prime movers in the setting up of the Midland Dairy Institute in 1895 on Belper's estate at New Kingston. This included a working dairy and as this expanded it required a regular supply of milk which came from the farms in Kingston, West Leake and East Leake – an important contribution to their economy for the next sixty years. From this small beginning came the Midland Agricultural College, now part of the University of Nottingham at its Sutton Bonington campus.

Farming continued as a major industry well into the twentieth century. Until the start of the Second World War, men and horses were the main source of power. Tractors and cars came into use gradually. Milking machines were being developed but were not entirely satisfactory. A national survey was carried out in 1940 - 41 to provide information of use in the direction of farming during the war. This survey showed that the nineteenth century farms were still in existence and that the numbers of farmers, landowners, farm workers and horses had not altered greatly. Some new crops had been introduced, mainly sugar beet and potatoes.

However, the war speeded up changes. Cars, lorries, tractors and milking machines came into general use and by 1950 horses had almost disappeared. There were fewer farmers as the smaller farmers tended to go out of farming. Their lands were taken over by the larger farmers, their houses and farm buildings were transformed into executive homes, and housing estates were built on the fields close to the village. In 1985 milk quotas were imposed by the European Economic Community. These set the quantity of milk which could be produced from each farm, requiring much more work in management. The smaller herds were sold, and the quotas were acquired by the bigger producers. In East Leake, as in much of this area, dairy herds were sold and the farmers switched to arable crops and to grassland for cattle and sheep. Today there are fewer farms, potatoes and sugar beet are no longer grown, and the farming has reverted to corn, cattle and sheep. Today very little milk is produced in East Leake. No farmers and very few farm workers live in the built-up area of the village. More farmhouses and buildings have been pulled down or converted to expensive houses whilst housing estates have been built on the home fields.

PART FIVE — INDUSTRIES OF EAST LEAKE

Weaving, lace and hosiery, basket making, gypsum and plaster, tradesmen and craftsmen

The forerunners of the industries of East Leake were the traders, fletchers (arrow makers), knitters, weavers and blacksmiths of the medieval town. As early as the fourteenth century there is mention of the Marcer or Mercer family, silk merchants, whilst among the frank pledgemen there was John Wyatt, a webster, a man involved in weaving. By the seventeenth century there were weavers, framework knitters, tailors, a blacksmith, a butcher and a mason. From now on, the village grew gradually as its existing families increased in size and developed the new industries.

WEAVING

In the late sixteenth and early seventeenth centuries there were three weavers in East Leake wealthy enough to leave wills. All three, Thomas Spenser, Burrows and Gervas Goulding, belonged to families found in the village throughout much of the medieval period.

The Bosworths were another family of weavers. From the early eighteenth century to 1841 they lived at Barn End in a timber-framed house on a corner plot between Castle Hill and Costock Road. They were farmers, probably of yeoman stock, and they were awarded 86 acres by the 1798 enclosure award. Thomas built a weaving shed close to the Baptist graveyard and later his son, also Thomas, converted this to a framework shop and built three cottages alongside. These are still there but the farmhouse and barns have been pulled down. The grandson, William, died in 1841 by which time weaving had ceased in East Leake.

As part of the weaving process, the cloths were washed and spread out to dry. This took place in Tenter Leys, a small field between Bosworth's farmstead and the Kingston Brook. The cloth was stretched between posts and held by iron tenter hooks – hence the expression "to be held on tenter hooks". Alas, a metal detector failed to find any in this field.

FRAMEWORK KNITTING — LACE AND HOSIERY

The making of lace and hose (stockings) were ancient hand crafts, mainly the work of the women of the family. In 1589, the Rev William Lee of Calverton in Nottinghamshire invented a knitting frame. It was not an immediate success and he and his brother James went to France to develop its use. About 1620 brother James returned to England and, in partnership with Aston, a miller at Thoroton in Nottinghamshire, improved the frame. This was a success and frames spread around Nottinghamshire during the next fifty years. It is probable that some were introduced to East Leake since an inhabitant in the late seventeenth century, Thomas Smith, who died in 1713, was a frame work knitter.

In the middle of the eighteenth century Thomas Clarke, a lace and hosier merchant, was living at Brickley on the Costock Road. He was a Baptist and made a significant impact on the development of the Baptist church in East Leake (p 24). He had business connections in Leicester and Nottingham and would have supplied the framework knitters with the wool and silk they required and purchased the lace and hose they produced. A deed of 1757 records a framework knitter at 10 - 12 Main Street. From this information it is reasonable to suppose that there were two small groups of framework knitters in East Leake in the middle of the eighteenth century.

One group was producing lace on bobbin net machines. These machines were expensive and their owners were men of means. Potter, in his history of East Leake in 1903, wrote that in living memory there were as many as twelve machines at work. White's Directory, 1832, names seven bobbin net makers — Thomas Bentley, Richard Flowers, Samson Gadd, John Hallam, Isaac James, William Neale and Samuel Smith. All were working in 1841 according to the census for that year and they or their sons and daughters were associated with lace making in 1851.

Bobbin net making declined during the 1840s and 1850s. Also during the 1840s and 50s, power driven lace machines in factories took over the production of lace. The East Leake manufacturers ceased to make lace but some had other businesses — Samson Gadd was also a miller and baker on the green, John Hallam was a publican at the Bulls Head and Isaac James was a carter and carrier. By the end of the 1860s lace making had ceased in East Leake.

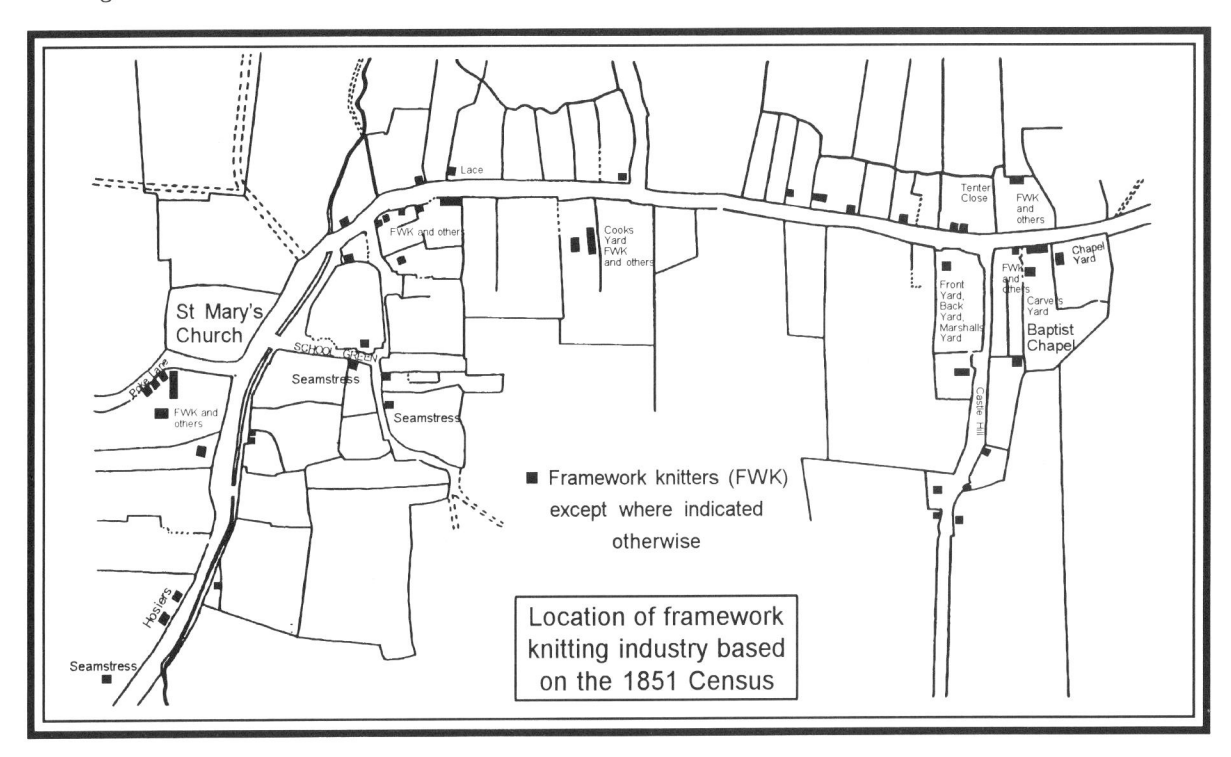

The Locations of the Framework Knitting Industry in East Leake

STOCKING FRAMES AND THE HOSIERY INDUSTRY

Some stocking frames were operating in the village during the eighteenth century and there may have been some increase into the next century. The major increase took place in the 1820s and the industry continued to expand until the middle of the nineteenth century when there were fourteen groups of knitters spread throughout the village.

A group consisted of from three to seventeen framework knitters, one of whom was a hosier arranging the purchase of the materials and the marketing of the stockings. They were housed in rows and yards of simple houses, one room up and one room down and the machines were housed in a shop (shed) built within the row or yard. The men-folk worked the machines and the women were seamers whilst the children helped with winding the wool. The families tended to continue together within each group and their descendants, Maltby, Doughty, Hallam, Savage, Croson and Marshall, are still living here, although their one-up-one-down houses are gone.

In the 1820s, 45 of the 58 houses built were in such rows and yards. Five groups of these were in the east end of the village inhabited by Baptists whilst there was one group of Anglicans on the green. The 1841 and 1851 census returns identify the hosiers and the origin of the framework knitters in each group.

Thus in Pecks Yard Row, opposite the Nags Head Inn there were William Reid, a hosier from Ireland, the Fosters from Costock, Haywoods from Bunny, Marshall from Eastwood, Harrison from Gotham and only the Cookes born in East Leake. William Reid and his son John were prominent elders of the Baptist Church.

Immediately east of Pecks Yard was Long Row. In 1851 William Gilbert, born in the village, is listed as a manufacturer of hosiery. George Hallam was born in Shepshed and this suggests he came to the village. The framework knitters were Gilbert, Osborne, Hallam, Savage and Croson, all born in East Leake.

In Carvers Yard between the Baptist Chapel and the Costock Road there were Archibald Reid from Dale (probably Deal) in Kent, Thomas Bentley a lacemaker, and the Neales, Newmans, Bentleys, Hallams and Ward born in the village.

On the village side of Castle Hill, in Back Yard, two rows of houses were built probably during the late eighteenth century and further rows were built during the 1820s. Most of the families in this area were village born but the hosiers amongst them included Hugh Maltby from Gotham and George Marshall from Granby, Leicestershire.

At the other end of the village on the Green there were William Ball from Barton, and Savage, Doughty and a Smith born in the village. Fourteen houses were built in each of the next two decades, most of these occupied by framework knitters.

A national survey of stocking machines recorded 119 in East Leake in 1844 and this indicates that each machine was operated by a particular knitter, they were not shared.

The industry continued to grow for another twenty years and a group of knitters came in from Gotham.

Edward Savage was a leading hosier from the 1820s to the 1860s. He came from a Leake family and was a prominent Anglican. There were a number of knitters in the west of the village and both he and his son had a store and yard in Brookside where they collected the stockings from the knitters in the Green, Brookside and Poke Lane (Station Road) area. His grandson, Frank Godber, recalled playing there.

The development of larger, steam-powered, machines was advancing factory production in towns such as Leicester and Loughborough. G H Angrave, a member of a leading land-owning and farming family in East Leake and Leicestershire, was a principal proprietor of a factory in Leicester. This family had taken no part in the framework knitting in East Leake. The rural villages could not provide the services for a factory and like many land-owning farmers of the times he invested his income in the town.

For a time the vested interests of the hosiers in the machine rentals which the framework knitters paid to use their machines had maintained their resistance to political power by the factory owners to abolish frame rentals. However, in 1874 an Act of Parliament abolished rentals and within thirty years most hand frames had ceased to be used. In East Leake the hosiers had become small manufacturers – thus in 1881 Richard Ball employed six men to work his machines and Edward Savage employed seven. Owen Stafford, Silas Maltby and Joseph Price were known as manufacturers. By 1891 the number of framework knitters had declined to 24. Twelve years later Potter wrote in his History of East Leake that only six frames were working. These were owned by Joseph Price in Chapel Yard, next to Carvers Yard. He was selling stockings in local street markets. Sadly he broke his neck in 1906 when pushing a basket of stockings to the railway station for sale at Sheffield. His brother William continued for a while at a store house behind Joyce's Manor (today the post office). By 1914 this had become a store for basket ware.

In the twentieth century a hosiery factory employing forty people was set up in Station Road by Briggs and Greenwood of Sutton-in-Ashfield but it has now closed.

BASKET MAKING

Willows or osiers have had many uses since very early times. Basket making was carried on in East Leake for 130 years from 1830 to 1960, part of an industry in the valleys of the Rivers Trent and Soar. It was organised on a family basis. The osier beds were planted by the men-folk on land adjoining rivers and streams, and with careful management they would last for fifty years. Cutting the rods was a skilled and laborious occupation carried out during the winter from November. The rods or withies were bunched and kept living standing in water pits. When they were required for use they were boiled in water tanks for eight to ten hours. Whilst they were still warm the skin was stripped off them by the women and children. They were used immediately or stored for sale or later use. Finally they were buffed by boiling to create the chestnut colour before being made up into many products such as baskets, hampers and furniture.

The Mills family were prominent basket makers throughout the Trent and Soar valleys. William and Sarah (née Withers) moved to West Leake about 1800 and their sons, John and William, settled in East Leake about 1830, when they were about thirty years old. Both were called skein basket makers. Skeins were produced by splitting the rods into three and trimming them ready for weaving.

John, the elder, had a house and workshop in Hardy's Yard on the east of the Green. His osier bed and water pits were on the side of the Sheepwash brook. His son, also John, joined him and with his widow in the 1850s continued the business. By 1881 they were employing six men and two boys. In 1885 John died and his son, Frederick Samuel, carried on for a while until his death in 1894.

William had a large corner plot on Main Street and the west side of Gotham Lane. It included his house, cottages and sheds. His osier beds and water pits were nearby on the side of the Kingston Brook. He developed this property, building cottages and the Beehive Works, including vats for boiling the rods used for making baskets and wicker ware. William Mills died in 1873. His son, Mark William, was a grocer and with his son, Walter Harry, a basket maker, carried on the business trading as "Mark W Mills, Art Cane, Wicker Furniture and Basket Manufacturer" at the Beehive Works.

By 1860 Matthew Mills, son of the youngest brother of John and William, had come from West Leake to set up as a basket maker in Main Street with osier beds between Kingston Brook and Costock Road. Later he was joined by his son, Felix William, trading as "Matthew Mills and Son, Fancy Basket and Wicker Work Makers, Wholesale and Export Family Basket Manufacturers".

In 1861 there were nine basket makers, assisted by their wives and children, working in the village.

Front cover of Mills catalogue

The industry now started to expand and in ten years had increased to 24 basket makers.

Framework knitting was declining and nine young men, including six from the village, had been apprenticed and in due course qualified as basket makers. About 1869 George Roulstone, his three sons and two brothers had come from Radcliffe-on-Trent to work for William Mills.

In the 1880s there was a major expansion in basket making in the village and the number of basket makers more than doubled to 54 men. Framework knitting had continued to decline and 25 young men under 25 years of age and born in East Leake had become basket makers. Two of these, the brothers Joseph and Frank Bramley set up in business. Joseph was farming at Brook Furlong and planted an osier bed by the brook. Frank was living in the Nook and built a work shed there.

In 1884 John Hugh Godber and his family of five, later increased to ten, came from Loughborough to set up in business as a basket maker and was joined by his sons. He and his elder sons, John and Thomas, moved back to Loughborough in the early 1900s whilst his other sons worked for Mark W Mills. One son, George, was in charge of the weavers. As well, he drew the pictures for a catalogue, an artistic achievement.

This group of basket makers was the basis of the industry in East Leake for the early part of the twentieth century. The leading firm was Mark W Mills and the proprietors succeeded from father to son, Walter Harry to Christopher Henry, and he to Christopher William. Whilst it was a family concern, it was a factory-style business.

The industry produced a wide range of furniture, hampers and baskets. Furniture catalogues illustrated easy chairs, ottomans, linen baskets and tables, providing a wide choice of well-designed, artistic furniture made by highly-skilled workers. Left-over materials were made into small articles such as work baskets and trays. Some of these have survived, particularly as treasured gifts. Factory and farm workers used small baskets for their sandwiches.

One of their products, eel traps, was modified for shell cases during the First World War, 1914 - 1918. There was a large Ordnance factory at Chilwell, just across the River Trent, producing shells for the big guns, known as "Big Berthas" used for the artillery barrages in France, and the eel traps were the right

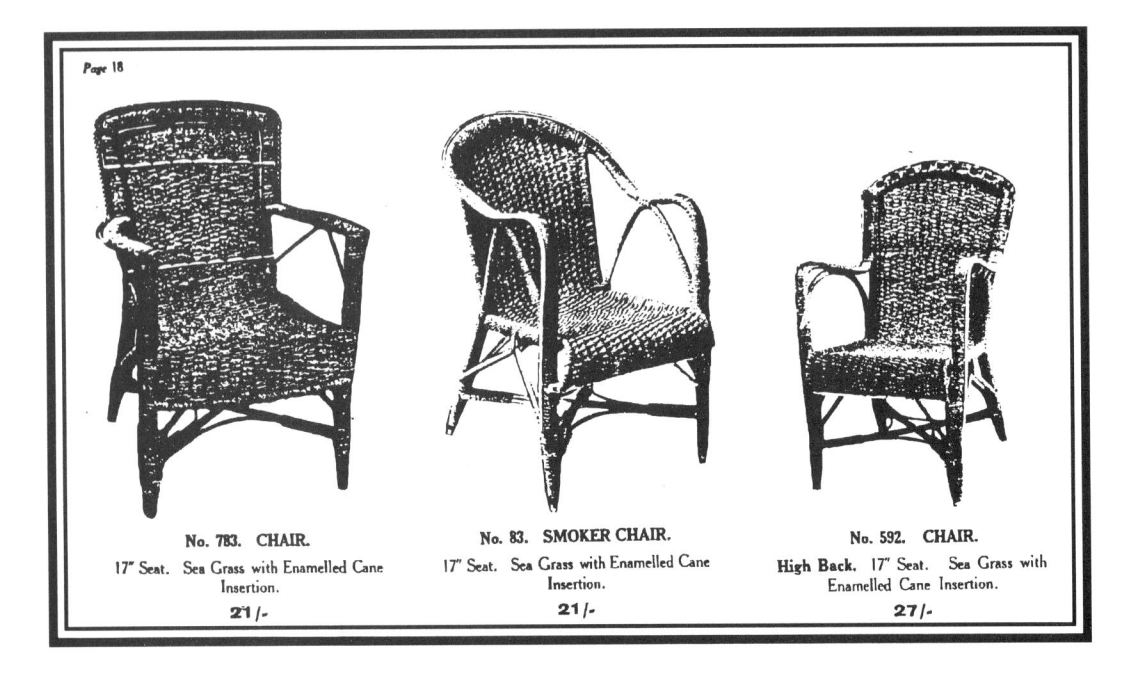

A Page from Mark W Mills catologue showing drawings by George Godber

size and shape to take the shells. Their production at East Leake was an important contribution to the war effort and it was marked by the award of badges to the workers. A photograph of 37 workers for Mark W Mills includes two shell cases in the foreground and lists the workers, a number of whom were the young basket makers named in the 1891 census.

After the war there was a national decline in basket making. Timber rods were replaced by metal, and wire replaced the skeins for furniture – this became familiar as "Lloyd Loom". Plastic was cheaper for baskets and hampers. Industrial development in the Far East produced cheap baskets and wicker ware. These three factors resulted in the decline of the industry in England from about 1930. Gradually the East Leake basket makers closed down. Although Mark W Mills produced a nominal catalogue in 1954, the business had virtually closed by 1960 and on the death of Christopher William Mills in 1965 the Beehive Works was sold to become a factory for plastic goods, but closed later.

GYPSUM AND PLASTER

Gypsum has been mined for plaster in East Leake for the past 125 years. It is a mineral form of calcium sulphate dihydrate and has many uses. In ancient times it was heated and ground for plaster to line walls. Another use in those times was as glass, being cut in thin slices. A translucent form was alabaster. It was found locally in Derbyshire at Chellaston and Fauld, and could be cut and polished and was widely used for monuments and tombs throughout the Saxon and Norman periods. But it was not used in the church at East Leake.

There were extensive deposits of gypsum about East Leake extending to the rivers Trent and Soar from Bunny and Stanford. Within the gypsum seams there are layers of ball gypsum, a pure form valuable for use in cosmetics, medicines and chemicals.

In the latter part of the nineteenth century the rising population and the expansion of industry required houses, factories and towns. This increased the demand for plaster by the building industry and plaster mines were opened in this area. The Rev Sneyd, curate in East Leake from 1874 to 1879, was concerned by the decline in the opportunities for young men in the village as the hosiery industry replaced the hand looms by power looms (p 42). He saw a plaster mine as a way of providing work for the young men and opened a mine in Rushcliffe. The remains of this mine are in a copse on the golf course, close to the clubhouse. According to the census for 1881 there were fourteen plaster miners in East Leake, probably all working in Sneyd's mine. In 1886 there was a decline in the building trade and this may have contributed to the closure of the mine.

In 1891 the Barnstone Lias and Cement Company opened a plaster mine on Hotchley Hill, opposite to Sneyd's mine. This mine was run by the Fowler Brothers, directors of the Barnstone Company and in 1891 they were employing six former employees of Sneyd. This mine was not successful and they opened a drift mine[5] nearby, the original Rushcliffe mine. According to Potter's history, they were employing thirty men in 1903 and became known as "Brothers Patent Plaster Company".

Plaster mining and manufacture in south west Nottinghamshire was affected by the need for power and coal to drive the grinding mills and heat the ground rock. The mills were powered by the River Soar at Zouch, near Hathern, and by the River Trent at Nottingham where railways could bring coal and transport the plaster. Mineral lines were built to the rivers. Access to Rushcliffe was difficult, and this may have contributed to the failure of both Sneyd's and Hotchley mines. However, in 1898 the position was relieved by the opening of the Great Central Railway passing through the Rushcliffe site. The Barnstone company, associated with the mines at both Gotham and Rushcliffe, supported the GCR. It built a mineral line from its Gotham works to the railway at Ruddington, and a goods depot at Rushcliffe. Within sixty years, road transport and power supplies of electricity and gas had replaced the

---

5. A drift mine is entered by walking or driving down a sloping shaft.

railway, closed in 1966 under the Beeching plan for British Railways (p 50).

In 1914 Mr O W Porritt, a Cumberland wool merchant, acquired the Brothers Company and registered it as Marblaegis Limited. He wished to call the plaster by a name descriptive of the product, derived from gypsum – a shield or protective coating. Already there was a plaster with a name incorporating these words. To avoid a risk of confusion and copyright he chose Marblaegis – from marble, a reference to alabaster, the marble-like gypsum rock used for carving and aegis, the Greek word for shield.

The first few years of the company were difficult as they coincided with the First World War, 1914 - 18, and a decline in the building industry.

After the war Capt Alexander Roulstone MC became mines manager. The Roulstone family came to East Leake as basket makers in the 1869s and he had served as a pilot in the Royal Flying Corps during the First World War.

Under Porritt and Roulstone, Marblaegis became a leading brand of plaster. In 1924 the company was purchased by a group of members of the Gypsum Association. The Association of Gypsum Manufacturers was formed in 1890 to provide agreement on prices and conditions of trade. It was not very effective and was dissolved in 1910. A year later the stronger and more effective Gypsum Association was formed and generally met at Derby. Capt Roulstone became one of the notable company representatives.

The new directors were all important men in the industry. Henry Newton, Chairman, was one of the Newtons who developed J C Staton & Co Ltd at Fauld, near Tutbury in Staffordshire. G John Germans, land agent, of Ashby de la Zouch, was a director of the Sub Wealden Company, based at Mountfield, Robertsbridge, Sussex and later a director of the Kingston mines. J J Shephard came from Gotham. His grandfather conducted a mining business at Redhill, Ratcliffe-on-Soar and his father took over a mine at Gotham. J J opened the Cuckoo Bush mine at Gotham in 1900. L C Kemp was a friend of the Newtons. In 1912 he visited the USA with Leigh Newton to get first-hand knowledge of the process of plaster manufacture. Later, in 1932, these two and Lord Belper (Kingston mines) visited Canada to study the manufacture of plasterboard. Rowland Ford was the son of Peter Ford who set up a mine at Fauld, alongside the Staton's mine.

Whilst all this was happening at Rushcliffe, plasterboard had been invented in the United States of America and increasingly replaced plaster as a building material. In 1890 Andrew Sachett encased the plaster mix in strong paper and produced boards on a fast-moving line. The boards were cut to standard lengths. From 1906 they became popular in the USA but the building industry in Britain was conservative. Gradually the prejudice was overcome and in 1917 British Plaster Board Ltd (BPB) was incorporated, the first directors being a bank manager, a solicitor, a builder and an American retarder manufacturer.

They erected a plasterboard plant at Wallasey, Cheshire, for the manufacture of Thistle baseboard. The demand grew and several companies set up manufacturing plants. BPB built a factory at Erith, Kent, using imported high-grade gypsum from Nova Scotia.

During the early 1930s the plaster industry was restructured by a series of amalgamations between the members of the Gypsum Association. BPB took the lead and acquired most of the companies in 1935 and 1936. Marblaegis was acquired in 1936. Several of the directors were important local persons: Lord Belper of Kingston, J N Derbyshire of Rempstone and J H Sheppard of Gotham.

The Marblaegis mine and plant continued as a leading producer of plaster. There was strong competition from cheaper plaster imported from the USA and Canada but these supplies were halted by the Second World War, 1939 - 1945. Production was increased at Rushcliffe. The labour force was augmented by prisoners of war, some of whom married local girls and stayed on. The former leader of the Berlin Philharmonic Orchestra drove the adit gear at one of the mines.

Following the expansion in 1935 - 36 BPB made important decisions about the future of the industry. It was decided to concentrate the production of plasterboard in Britain at Rushcliffe where there were large deposits of gypsum rock, especially suitable for the plaster used for boards. The deposits extended under the eastern side of East Leake and under the hills from Cuckoo Bush at Gotham to the Old Wood at Bunny. The

Rushcliffe mine and plant was not the best point at which to site the mine in relation to the deposits but the development of lorries, tractors and cars overcame this and an underground road system was constructed.

Implementation of these changes was delayed by the Second World War, 1939 - 1945 after which the Marblaegis mine was reconstructed. A new adit was built over the old one and modern mining equipment, as used in coal mining, was installed. The work was completed by 1947 and the mine became the largest producer of rock in the East Midlands.

A new plant for the production of plasterboard was built in 1946 - 47 at a cost of over three quarters of a million pounds. It was the most advanced plant in Europe and the output of board from the line outstripped that of any other factories. The plant, mine and other activities at Rushcliffe operated from now on as British Gypsum Ltd within the parent company, British Plaster Board Ltd, later BPB Industries PLC. BPB closed down the production of plaster at Wallasey and transferred the production at Rushcliffe to the Gotham works.

Since 1947 there has been continuous expansion to meet the demands of the growth in the construction industry. By 1952 the demand for plasterboard was such that British Gypsum could no longer boast of its ability to meet supply deadlines and a second supply line was installed with half the capacity of the first. This was upgraded by 1964 to the same capacity as the first.

BPB was in a strong position to meet the increasing demands for plaster and gypsum products. Towards the end of 1933 Philip Derbyshire, son of J N Derbyshire, persuaded the Gotham Company to appoint a chemist, Leslie Haddon. From this the Research and Development Division (R & D) evolved and eventually moved to the Rushcliffe site. The division developed new uses for board. One such, Paramount dry partitioning, provided an easy and quick method of installing internal partitions and in 1956 a fully-mechanised panel plant was set up at Rushcliffe and this became one of its staple products. Later a fire-resistant plaster was developed and a plant was set up in 1975.

By the early 1960s the demand for plasterboard had outstripped the production at Rushcliffe and three new plants with the latest technology had been built elsewhere. However, in 1979 a massive new investment was started at Rushcliffe. A third board line was completed by 1983 and the first line was taken out. A fourth line was completed in 1984 and in December the last sheet of plasterboard rolled off the second line. Now Rushcliffe was producing forty per cent of the total production of British Gypsum Ltd. Weekly production of these new lines was 1.3 million m^2 of board, 85 per cent more than the 700,000 m^2 produced by the first two lines.

A feature of the countryside for many years had been the film of gypsum dust to the north of the plant. It was a harmless pollutant; indeed, ground gypsum was a soil conditioner. About this time special controls were introduced and dust no longer disfigures the countryside.

R and D had developed substantial improvements in the equipment used to calcine gypsum powder prior to its use in product manufacture. The Division received the Queen's Award for Technological Achievement in 1988 in recognition of this work.

The gypsum at the Glebe Mine, Gotham, was exhausted and was replaced by the discovery and subsequent development of fresh gypsum reserves at Barrow.

Gypsum is now produced as a result of the installation of pollution abatement equipment at the Ratcliffe Power Station. This is now used in substantial quantities to produce plasterboard.

For a time the head offices were moved from London to nearby Ruddington. In 1993 they relocated to a first-class purpose-built office building at Rushcliffe. BPB PLC eventually developed as an international organisation, becoming one of the world's largest producers of gypsum building materials.

British Gypsum at Rushcliffe has been the flagship of BPB with the most advanced plant of its kind. It has always been proud of its boast to deliver a high standard of service to the industry.

PART SIX — MODERN TIMES

Local government, education, Poor Law, National Health Service, census, land ownership, the Great Central Railway and the last fifty years

During the nineteenth century changes in Great Leake followed the national pattern. There was a considerable increase in the population and whilst many were employed in the expanding industries there was an increase not only in the total but also in the proportion of craftsmen, shopkeepers and others. A peak population of 1148 is recorded in the 1851 census; 252 were employed in the industries of farming, lace, hosiery and basket-making. This does not include the contribution of women and children. There were 101 in other occupations providing for the general needs of the community:

- 38 in clothing, mainly dressmakers, tailors and shoemakers
- 34 craftsmen such as bricklayers, carpenters, blacksmiths and millers
- 21 shopkeepers, ie grocers, butchers, bakers, coal sellers and innkeepers
- 8 others — curate, policeman, nurse, school mistress, artist, post mistress and two carriers.

By 1891 the numbers employed in clothing had halved, as dressmaking, tailoring and shoemaking moved into factories supplying town shops. One tailor left the village and set up a factory making suits. The decline in the number of craftsmen included seven millers as the flour milling industry moved towards large mills.

An increase in government participation in life – Board Schools, police, taxation, registration of births, marriages and deaths – is reflected in the occupations involved.

There were eight charwomen in 1891. In previous census returns they had not been recorded as such. Whilst census returns for the twentieth century are not yet available in the detail of those in the nineteenth century, the pattern in 1891 did not change much in East Leake for the next fifty years.

Farm labourers, farm and house servants are recorded under various names in the nineteenth century census returns. As standards of living rose they were an important part of life in the homes of the nobility and gentry, the well-off such as the yeomen and farmers who employed them. Frequently they were hired on a yearly or half-yearly basis at hiring fairs such as those in Great Leake. Hirings were held on the patronal festival day – for St Leonard's this was 7th November. In 1832 White's Directories record four hirings a year – Candlemass Day (2nd February), the first and last Fridays in November. By 1844 they were reduced to three in each year. By the end of the nineteenth century hirings had ceased.

Hirings were at their height about 1848 - 50 when large crowds of servants were gathered for more than 200 yards in the main street, in the road from the church to Bley School and in the road to West Leake.

A servants' register for the parish of East Leake includes nine entries of servants hired on 11th November 1818 for 51 months. A memorandum book kept by William Braithwaite of Welldales Farm records hirings of farm labourers in 1872 - 74.

EDUCATION

Free education for poor boys and girls was provided by the school founded and endowed by John Bley in 1724. By the late eighteenth century the need for education had increased. Until then it had been a function of the church. In 1824 under the rector, Rev Holcomb, the Anglican church built a schoolroom on the glebe land to the east of the church and, under the Rev Bateman, extended it in 1850. The curate organised evening classes mainly for young adults. The non-conformists set up Sunday Schools needed to educate their children. The Baptists started in a private house in 1807 and included a schoolroom in the extension to the church in 1809. The Wesleyan Methodists set up

Sunday Schools in their first church, and when they built a new church in 1863 continued to use their first church as a schoolroom.

In accordance with the Elementary Education Act of 1870, the East Leake School Board was formed in 1874, and the Board agreed to carry on the charity set up by John Bley, taking over the property and endowments. The school house deteriorated and was demolished. The Wymeswold lands were sold and the money put towards the cost of a new school built behind Bley's school.

While the Board School was being built, accommodation was rented in the church schoolroom and the Three Horseshoes Inn. The Board School was opened on 29th June 1875. Mr W Shannon was the schoolmaster with his wife and there were eighty school children. Initially there was only one room with an infant gallery. Rooms were added, including a house for the headmaster. It was extended in 1905 when it became an elementary school.

THE CARE OF THE POOR

In the eighteenth and early nineteenth centuries there was a workhouse on the Green. The house is still standing on the corner between the Nook and the yard of the Three Horseshoes Inn. In 1794 the keeper, Charles Cross, took over from Richard Garner three flock beds, three bedsteads, bed linen, a table and cooking utensils.

An act in 1834 formed a central authority, the Poor Law Commission, empowered to issue orders for regulating the local administration of poor relief. East Leake was one of 25 parishes in south-west Nottinghamshire and north Leicestershire included in the Loughborough Union. A workhouse was built in Derby Road, Loughborough, and the East Leake house was closed. W J Tunnicliffe was appointed as a relieving officer in East Leake and John Bostock of Costock as medical officer.

Potter records 162 persons in Friendly Societies in 1815. These enabled the members to accumulate funds to meet the expenses of funerals, sickness, old age and such like personal expenses, a necessary form of insurance before the 1912 Pension and later the Welfare State.

GREAT CENTRAL RAILWAY

East Leake was on the route of the last major rail line to be built to London in the nineteenth century. Sir Edwin Watkins realised that his line from Manchester and Sheffield to Lincolnshire needed a link to London and he was unable to arrange the use of existing main lines. He was interested in establishing a direct link between Liverpool and Paris through London and the proposed Channel Tunnel. In 1891 he obtained parliamentary approval for a line from Sheffield through South Yorkshire, Nottinghamshire, Leicestershire, Northamptonshire and Quainton Road, Buckinghamshire. Much of the line south of Leicester ran through thinly populated rural areas. Locally it ran from Nottingham Victoria through Wilford, Ruddington and East Leake to Loughborough Central. A branch line from Ruddington to Gotham and sidings at Rushcliffe served the plaster works at Gotham and East Leake. The building of Barnstone Tunnel, south of East Leake, found very good quality blue lias stone and a company was formed to erect lime kilns and a private siding. This was a successful enterprise for a number of years. The whole line was built by seven contracts, one boundary between adjoining contracts being at Rushcliffe.

A station and goods yard were built at East Leake and the first passenger trains ran in 1898. In 1911 a halt was opened at Rushcliffe. Initially there were seven down trains and ten up trains (down trains from London; up trains to London) the journey to London taking about three hours. By 1922 there were 15 down trains and 13 up trains. The fastest train was "The Master Cutler" from Sheffield to

London in the morning, and London to Sheffield in the late afternoon, approximately two and a half hours.

In 1923 the Great Central Railway was incorporated in the London and North Eastern Railway and nationalised in 1948.

During the Second World War the central control office was moved from Nottingham to a bomb-proof building at East Leake station. One air raid attempted to cut the two main lines at Sutton Bonington and East Leake.

A review of the viability of lines, the Beeching plan, decided to close the Great Central Railway, and the last train at East Leake was on 3rd May 1969. Thus the last main line built to London was the first to close. Within thirty years the Channel Tunnel had been bored and was operating. Sir Edwin Watkins's concept had been justified. Doubtless in the not-too-distant future there will be direct lines from the Midlands and North of England to Paris.

The coming of the railway in 1898 and the growth in the two industries of plaster and basket making reversed the decline in the population that had taken place in the latter half of the nineteenth century.

The railway provided employment and the company built a station master's house at the station as well as a terrace of four houses nearby. At the same time it attracted people to live here and commute to work in Nottingham and Loughborough. This attraction was augmented in 1926 when the Dabells of Gotham set up the South Notts Bus Company providing a frequent service between Loughborough and Nottingham. Nottingham business and professional men built large houses on either side of the station from which they could reach their offices within half an hour. Some were known for dashing to the station in their slippers. Mills, the basket-making family, extended housing on Woodgate Road. After the first World War, 1914 - 18, Capt Roulstone invested in housing, initially with ex-army wooden huts adjoining the plaster works and later by in-filling. In the mid-1930s Basford Rural District developed council housing in the triangle between Kirk Ley Road and Woodgate Road.

By 1941 the population had risen to 1500 from the low level of 850 in 1901. Many of these were descendants of the families living here in the nineteenth century and earlier. There had been a slight increase in the inhabited area, but the major change was in its appearance and in the facilities. Even the main street was still rolled stone and gravel in 1900. Within a few years, with the exception of three or four little-used track ways, the roads were macadamised and drained and the footpaths in the built-up areas were tarred. Some street lighting had been installed. Mains water, sewerage and drainage were provided in the 1930s. The introduction of cars and lorries required garages, and a large haulage business developed from Hardstaff's, a carrier's business. Some old properties had been replaced, but it was still the "same" village. Only one new public building had been erected, the Village Hall in 1935. This owed much to the Women's Institute, the Rector Rev R C Smith, and village note-worthies.

LOCAL GOVERNMENT – THE PARISH COUNCIL

From the earliest Saxon times the administration in villages and towns has been by a committee or council, for much of the time called a vestry. In medieval times the vestry consisted of the landowners (people with independent rights to land) bonded to attend the meetings. The lords of the manor were the leaders. There were several tiers of civil administration – hundreds, counties, lords of areas or kingdoms and ultimately the king. Initially there were several kingdoms.

This history tells of the ways in which they operated and their responsibilities. As the political and social scene changed central government increased its powers, directing courts of justice, registration of land ownership and occupation, births, marriages and deaths, wills, and care of the poor. The administration of the church was separate but carried out many of these activities.

The development of world trade, the industrial and agricultural revolution and the increase in the population added to the scale of civil administration. At the same time Parliament was taking over the powers of government. The lords of the manor and the vestries were decreasing in importance. In particular, enclosure did away with the work of the lord of the manor and the vestry in controlling the day-to-day management of the common fields.

The process of creating a proper framework of local government in England took most of the nineteenth century to achieve. To post-feudal arrangements in ancient towns and cities were added the major industrial city corporations and town councils, then Disraeli's 1880 Local Government Act created their country counterparts the county and district councils. Finally the Liberal H H Fowler introduced a Bill giving considerable powers to a new tranche of minor authorities, secular parish councils which would take over from the parochial vestry system all non-ecclesiastical functions together with new practical responsibilities.

Tory opposition watered down the proposed revenue-raising powers to the extent that the 1894 Local Government Act (known as the Parish Councils Act) only permitted councils to collect a 3d rate, with another 3d for really exceptional expenditure. Even as late as 1928, this had only risen to a 4d rate plus another exceptional 4d, rather less in real terms than the 1894 level; this suggests that the limitation imposed in the first place had had its desired effect.

In East Leake the Act was put into effect on 31st December 1894 when the Rector, Rev Potter, convened a meeting at which the first Parish Council was elected. The work of the Parish Council is described in Part Seven.

THE LAST FIFTY YEARS 1948 - 1998

During the Second World War nation-wide consideration had been given to the plans for the future development of towns, villages and the countryside. It was decided to expand East Leake to a centre for public services such as schools, a library, a health centre and an eventual increase in the population from 1500 to 6000. This was maintaining its historical position as a civic centre of the south west corner of Nottinghamshire.

An important factor in this decision was the policy of British Plaster Board in 1936 to set up its head offices at its Rushcliffe site and to build a plant to supply plasterboard for the whole country. The war delayed the setting up of the plant until after its conclusion. There was an urgent need for housing for the extra workers required and a housing estate was built on the Gotham Road between the Rushcliffe works and the main street. Cheap and easily erected prefabricated houses had been designed to provide short-term accommodation for the families bombed out during the war, and the Basford Rural District Council selected them. Their expected life span was ten years, but fifty years later they are still occupied, having been improved from time to time. The use of aluminium gave rise to the unpleasant and unpopular name of "Tin Town" being used for this Rushcliffe Estate. After this the council built more houses in the triangle between Kirk Ley Road and Woodgate Road.

In accordance with government policy, many of the lower grade houses built between the mid-eighteenth century and 1850 were cleared. On some of the cleared plots modern houses were erected, whilst the western side of Castle Hill and part of the Green became amenity sites.

Housing estates have developed since 1950 and will continue to do so in the future. Most of them have been close to the original built-up area about Main Street, School Green, Brookside, Woodgate, Station Road and West Leake Road. The only extension beyond this has been on either side of Gotham Road between Rushcliffe and the brook by Stonebridge. Most of these estates have been on the fields close to the village farmsteads. These became available as the farms were no longer in use as a result of the changes in farming (p 30).

In the 1950s the centre of the village was redeveloped. Gotham Road was widened to a double track and shops built on both sides. On the west side a car park and playing fields were formed beyond the shops. Opposite, on the east side, a civic centre was developed including a fire station, a county library and a health centre. The new shops extended eastward in Main Street from its junction with Gotham Road. In 1997 a Co-op superstore was built in Main Street on the site of Hardstaff's haulage company.

Public buildings were too small for the much larger population. The only school sufficed for a while. The school system was being changed and the leaving age raised. In 1952 an infants' school was opened in Lantern Lane. An aluminium building like the Rushcliffe Estate, it was destroyed by a fire in 1995. The old school continued as the secondary school for the older children until 1956 when the new Harry Carlton Secondary School, next to Lantern Lane Primary School was opened. The school was named after a notable public figure. This became the Harry Carlton Comprehensive School with an associated sports and community centre. As the village grew, further accommodation was required for younger children. Lantern Lane Primary was extended, whilst the old village school, renamed Brookside, was extended on the original site by a new school in 1966 with an annexe on Brookside in 1975. Numbers declined, this annexe was closed, and a small housing estate built on the field in which the annexe had been built. The road through this estate was named Leivers Close, after Dan Leivers, the headmaster of the village school from 1924 to 1951.

Likewise, the churches have had to meet the demands of a larger population. There are difficulties in adding to ancient churches, and so far the church itself has not been able to extend. Both the Anglicans and the Baptists have extended their schoolrooms. The Methodists decided to replace their rather cool and uninviting Victorian church in April 1983 by a modern, multi-purpose building. The main hall serves as church schoolroom and a general purposes room. The old church was demolished and the site is now a garden.

The expansion of the population brought in outsiders, some of whom were Catholics. Along with Catholics in neighbouring villages they had to travel to Loughborough to hear Mass. They were encouraged by Father Hogan of Loughborough to raise funds and build a church in East Leake on a plot of land given by Captain Alexander Roulstone, MC, and his wife – neither of them Catholics. The church, Our Lady of the Angels, was opened in May 1955. It was designed by Mr E Bower Norris of Stafford, a well-known Catholic ecclesiastical architect. In the first place it was served by local Rosminian priests from Loughborough and Ratcliffe College, and in 1969 it was taken over by the Catholic Diocese of Nottingham, East Leake becoming an independent parish within the diocese.

In the last fifty years East Leake has become a residential village, many of the people working away from home. The largest local employer is British Gypsum Limited at Rushcliffe. Members of staff at the five universities at Nottingham, Loughborough and Leicester, East Midlands Airport, Ratcliffe Power Station and the National Westminster Bank have been attracted to the village. Their children are likely to include a proportion of potentially more intelligent pupils with parents keen that they should receive a good education. All three schools have a high reputation. The village has proved attractive to retired people, parents of the younger couples. Also there is a core of descendants of old village families.

No longer do the local industries, farming, framework knitting, basket-making provide employment for most of the inhabitants. Mills basket wares and British Plaster Board carried the name of East Leake to distant countries. In the last fifty years, two firms have started in East Leake – bell ropes to ring cathedral bells in distant countries and a nursery producing rose and oak plants using new methods.

In 1973 there were changes in connection with Taylor's Bell Foundry in Loughborough. An East Leake man, Alfred Ellis, started a tent and rope making business in East Leake, renting the war time control building of the Great Central Railway, eminently suitable as it had a long, clear length of space. It is one of four bell rope manufacturers in the country. GCR sold the goods yard including the control centre in 1987 and Alfred Ellis moved to a purpose-built factory about a mile away on the outskirts of Costock.

Ropes had been made in East Leake by the Tafts. The first rope walk was alongside the brook in front of their cottage and paddocks at Nos 1 - 3 Brookside. The business flourished as it was just where the hirings were held. When the hirings were no longer held the business ceased to be profitable and Thomas Taft sold it to his son-in-law, William Hardy. He closed it shortly afterwards.

About 1982 Dr and Mrs Wright set up in business in East Leake, producing roses by micro-propagation. Conventional methods of producing plants from cuttings and seeds do not result in genetic copies of the original plant. As part of their studies at Nottingham University School of Agriculture at Sutton Bonington, the Wrights had been involved in research into cloning, propagation from single cells. At the same time they applied their methods to overcome the difficulties in propagating oaks, particularly the famous Major Oak of Sherwood Forest. They have been successful in producing saplings just in time, as the old tree is dying. In 1998 saplings were being sold for planting in Sherwood Forest and in the USA.

Seven thousand years ago nomads cut down areas of primeval forest to provide settled homesteads and land for cultivating crops to provide food for man and livestock. For most, maybe all of this time, man has lived on the spot where he settled, and today these oak saplings are being grown here to replace the oaks needed to maintain the ancient Sherwood Forest which originally stretched throughout the Trent and Soar valleys.

Two old pictures of the same stretch of Main Street

In the view on the left, looking east, the gable end of the cottages that were pulled down to make room for the village hall car park is on the left side of the road. The next visible building is the Wesleyan Chapel and beyond that is the Beehive Works. In the view on the right, which is looking west, the front of the old Methodist Church can just be seen on the left side of the road. Opposite is the Wesleyan Chapel and the cottages that originally stood on the site of the village hall.

PART SEVEN — THE PARISH COUNCIL

Entirely derived from the Minute Books of the Council
By Mollie Jacques

In East Leake, the 1894 Parish Councils Act was put into effect on 31st December; 1894, when Rev Sidney Potter convened a meeting in the Board School, at which the following were elected to serve as the village's first Parish Council:

Ezra Pidcock (Chairman)
George Blower
Henry Smith
Mark W Mills
G H Angrave
Matthew Mills (Treasurer)
John Pierrepoint
John Brown
Edward Savage
William Sharp
Edwin Mills (Clerk)

The Council had a number of clear responsibilities which were addressed immediately. The duties of the Poor Law Union overseers were transferred directly to the new council and Oswald Kirk was appointed collector of the poor rate; there was a "waywarden" to survey and report on local highways, and a "sanitary" committee to keep an eye on the condition of paths and water courses and drains.

The council had two sources of income, the rates and rents from letting the "herbage" of lanes on the village outskirts. Rates related to the various government boards which had been the Victorian way of tackling problems, so were identified according to specific need such as the "poor rate" or the "sanitary rate" (for collecting which Oswald Kirk in 1895 requested and was granted an additional £2 per annum). In 1896, a new rating formula was introduced, so that the total assessment of the village dropped from £3947 to £3780. Though significant, this reduction was clearly not a problem, because the council only precepted for 1½d rate, giving an income of £20 (Appendix 3). At the same meeting, they decided to take on what was to become the major task and preoccupation of their first half century.

In April 1896 the council adopted the 1833 Lighting and Watch Act, under which they were empowered to raise a rate to install and maintain street lights, agreeing upon the maximum special rate of 3d. The story of East Leake's lights is worth tracing in some detail, because it reveals how modern amenities must have come to many a rural area, innovation being treated firstly with suspicion and only later with enthusiasm, but also, sadly, how a chronic reluctance to spend money can lead to lost opportunities.

A minute for 27th July 1896 tells of a decision to purchase six lamps and brackets for Main Street at £1 10s 0d per lamp and 10s 6d per bracket (£12 3s 0d); William Cousins, lamplighter, to be employed at £1 5s 0d pa; William Bramley to make a suitable ladder (10s 6d). Lamps were to be lit from 1st October to 31st March, and the council were to buy a barrel of best American oil, together with taps and a key.

In August 1897, oil cost 6d per gallon from Moores of Loughborough or 5½d from Walter Mills of East Leake, and Mr Cousins's pay rose to 5s 0d per week for the season (in 1898 it rose to 6s 0d). Inflation in 1899 meant oil cost 8d per gallon and Cousins had to have 7s 0d per week. "... the lights are to be put out every night at 10 o'clock except Saturday, then 11 o'clock, and to be lighted every night with the exception of 5 before and 5 after the full moon ... the Clerk to have the power to order the lamps to be lighted on dull and foggy nights when he thought it necessary".

In 1910, best "Royal Daylight" oil cost only 5¼d per gallon, but by 1913 it was again over 7d. Also in 1910, there was a great debate about the relative merits of oil and coal gas. Oil was decided to be more economical, so Cumberland & Hobbs was commissioned to erect three experimental lamps at their cost, council to pay for the oil.

On 13th October 1914, a decision was taken to convert to a new system which could light homes as well as streets, but then it was realised there was not enough money, so on 4th April 1915 it was agreed to have no lighting till the war was over (NB this is the first reference in the minutes to World War I). There seemed to be a sense of satisfaction that no rate would need to be levied. Because of alarms about cost, the decision to re-light the village was not taken until March 1922, when a resumption of the 3d rate was agreed.

Two schemes for electric lighting were considered in late 1922. Melton Mowbray Electric Supply Co. Ltd was too expensive, but Mr Porritt (of Rushcliffe Lodge) had a system for his estate which might be joined. The lighting rate was suspended while this was looked into, but when this, too, was found to be too costly, it was decided to await development of the Central Electric Lighting Scheme. The old paraffin lamps were disposed of, and the village remained dark.

At last, in 1928, council agreed to seek an estimate from the Derbyshire & Nottinghamshire Electric Co of Ilkeston. Terms of £4 10s 0d per lamp per annum, using existing standards (£1 per standard to shift them) were put to a parish meeting for approval. In 1929 the conversion and illuminating of twelve lamps cost £76 16s 0d; this was only along Main Street and in the village centre.

6th November 1931, re what is now Rushcliffe Grove: " ... Mr Porritt was willing to give a lamp to the parish provided they maintained the lighting of same. As the lamp was suggested being put over the entrance to the bungalows, this being on private property, was not favoured by the council, who suggested a lamp should be erected immediately outside the entrance which would give a light to Gotham Road, Bunny Road and also the bungalow road. The chairman remarked he did not think this would be favoured by Mr Porritt". Another disputed area was the station approach – who would pay? Mr Harry Carlton went to London to see the chief engineer, but failed to convince him of the railway company's obligation, though he warned him that "people would not patronise the railway if inadequately lit, when the buses passed their door". The Town Lands Trust came to the rescue, offering five lamps to cover both sites. By 1934, a 6d rate (permitted under an Act of 1931) was required to meet the lighting bill. All street lights were put out in 1939 when World War II started. The minutes do not record the exciting time when they went on again. 1949 – the council had to approach EMEB to get street lights for the new Rushcliffe estate. In 1959, council agreed to Basford Rural District Council's recommendation that lighting services should be consolidated and parish councils' individual powers under the 1833 Act should be relinquished. Separate lighting rates were still levied, however – £605 (1960), £344 (1961), £609 (1962) until the end of March 1962, when Basford RDC finally took over.

Other modern amenities which we take for granted these days are sewage disposal and the supply of fresh water. The first, along with street cleaning and the maintenance of water-courses, was the statutory responsibility of the rural district council (Leake RDC until 1934 when the much larger Basford RDC was created) and over the years there are many examples of the council having to complain about filthy streets and over-flowing drains.

A lengthy discussion on 21st July 1926 is described, when it was agreed to ask Leake RDC to see to dyke emptying in frosty weather, because in hot weather the process was "more than a scent bottle" (Arthur Wass, Clerk). In 1931, "urban" powers became available to parish councils, to do with "scavenging", refuse disposal and other sanitary measures, but as a special rate would be required East Leake Parish Council declined the opportunity. In 1957, the County Council offered to devolve to the parish its 1902 Open Spaces Act power to manage the village brook; council entered into discussions with the Kingston Brook Internal Drainage Board, but soon declined this opportunity also.

Water supply was somewhat different, in that it seems the Parish Council could always have become involved in the expense of installing a piped system, but on several occasions it decided against it. Leake RDC tried to interest it in a scheme for piping water in 1914, but it replied expressing "their entire satisfaction with the present supply". In 1923, Mr Porritt was supplying all his estate houses with pure drinking water. It was agreed to approach him for any surplus to come East Leake's way "before another certain village in the vicinity" (which village, one wonders?), but shortly afterwards it appeared that Mr Porritt's estate was for sale, so the idea was aborted. In 1929, a much bigger scheme was put to a parish meeting:

The Parish Council

Loughborough Corporation, jointly with Leake RDC (representing Belton, Hathern, Long Whatton, East Leake, Normanton and Sutton Bonington), proposed to provide mains water for the whole area, taking a 27 year loan of £51,038 for the purpose. It would mean a 2s 6d rate for the consumer – with 9s 0d per annum extra for a bath. Kirk Lea, Station Road, Main Street, Costock Road and Castle Hill would be served. A commotion ensued from Gotham Road residents, who already had water; they said it would not be fair to pay for water they would not enjoy. They insisted that a poll should be taken. Mr Sands thought that people who really required water should pay more, seeing that "the poorer classes could ill afford to contribute towards something they did not require". ... East Leake did not get its water.

In June 1932, Mr Porritt's agent approached Harry Carlton again, offering plant and machinery for £500. As the Parish Council had insufficient powers to go solo on this, they passed the matter on, urgently, to Basford RDC. The council meeting of 9th August was acrimonious. Some said Poritt's water had been condemned in 1929; others, that it had been approved for drinking purposes; the RDC's reply gave no cheer – the Parish Council had rejected the earlier Loughborough proposals on the grounds of excessive cost and the satisfactory quality of East Leake well water. Therefore they were not keen on the Porritt scheme and the charges for joining with Loughborough would now be even higher. Characteristically, council decided to wait and see. In July 1934, it finally agreed to accept the Loughborough scheme and had the nerve to ask Basford RDC to expedite matters! In February 1936, a grant of £6,125 was agreed with Basford, and East Leake got piped water at last. Also in that year, a joint sewerage scheme with Costock was approved.

The Parish Council always stoutly defended the village in two other important local government functions, housing (district and borough council) and education (county council after 1902). Perhaps it is significant that the parish itself would never be called upon to provide or visibly pay for either of these; it confidently found its voice when its budget was not under threat.

The village got its first municipal housing in the aftermath of World War I when, in March 1919, Leake RDC proposed a scheme of twenty properties. Council responded by asking for forty, and engaged vigorously in discussing sites. It did not favour Castle Hill, which was first suggested by the RDC, and instead proposed Gotham Road south of Lantern Lane, West Leake Road or Kirk Lea, the RDC's choice finally falling on Kirk Lea.

During the '20s and '30s there was considerable activity nationally in updating or demolishing and replacing some of the ancient, insanitary village dwellings which were seen as no longer fit to live in, and council negotiated with both county and district at various times. There was some anxiety over the 1926 Housing (Rural Workers) Act under which financial assistance was available to property owners for re-conditioning houses. It was felt (by owners) that there might be too many restrictions attached.

Conversely, in 1937, council expressed concern over Basford's plans to re-house elderly tenants from sub-standard, but very cheap, old cottages and urged the building of low-rent bungalows. It was pointed out that a couple on old age pension received only £1 per week and that a rent of 6s 0d would be beyond them.

In 1938, council complained to Basford that only twenty two out of a proposed sixty houses had been built; the RDC replied that another 11.4 acres of land had now been secured and forty to sixty houses would soon be up.

In January 1945, before World War II was actually over, council was debating the needs of the village. It wanted more houses, but not on an extended Kirk Lea estate – which is where, of course, it got fifty of them, but no elderly persons' bungalows, and even at this late date only some properties had electric sockets. Pressure on tenancies was fierce and complaints that a non-East Leake family had moved in were only calmed when the RDC explained its obligation to re-house bombed-out families.

The large Rushcliffe estate known as "Tin Town" arrived on the scene in 1948, after great difficulties in persuading Mr Barkus to sell the land to Basford RDC. There are many references to this, and also to subsequent problems with tenancy allocations. Mr Crosland, one of the East Leake representatives on the RDC, precipitated some heated argument by allegedly trying to keep the allocations in his gift. This development added over 200 houses to the village.

By 1960 the next great push was on. Oldershaw Road was built, the Stonebridge estate was just being started, and the county council announced its predictions for the expansion of East Leake to 4000 population by 1971 and 6000 by 1975. That meant 500 more dwellings, twelve shops, light industry, improved education and health services and so on. Council was understandably anxious about the strains all this would impose on the village infrastructure.

For several years at this period, there had been a stream of complaints about disconcertingly variable voltage in the electricity supply which EMEB seemed to be nowhere near correcting, and there were, as ever, fears that the barely adequate sewerage system would fail.

During the '60s, most local housing development was in the private sector, and the Parish Council, having no planning powers, could only try to see that good practice was followed. It has to be said that some planning "givens" of the '60s and '70s, for instance the allowance of 1 acre of open space per hundred dwellings, could not have been better designed to cause problems for those, ie the Parish Council, who would have to sort out future maintenance. The council could, however, take part in consultation with the County Council in 1966 over the planned development of the village centre.

It briefly looked as if council might achieve a coherent complex of community centre, library, health centre, even an assembly room in the area behind the village hall, but government financial limits prevented such luxury. At least the building of another pub and a petrol station in the area where the fire station now stands was prevented. Local authority building became more varied as time went by, and the parish council was supportive both of residents who were hostile to the original designs and of Rushcliffe Borough Council (the successor, in 1974, to Basford RDC) which was charged with providing suitable accommodation for the elderly, when Tutin Court was developed in the late '70s. Even more recently, the mixed development at Meeting House Close received full council backing.

When it came to education, council's attitude was clear from the beginning. It responded as soon as asked to appoint managers when the new education committee took over the old Board School in 1902, and throughout has supported all state education requirements. On 8th June 1903, it waded in thus regarding the County Council's proposals in implementing the 1902 Act:

"The meeting condemns the present plan of the sites committee to enlarge the present school premises, but [urges them] to consider the building of a new school". On 8th June 1904, it was reported that Messrs Pidcock and Kirk had resigned as school managers over the County Council's decision on the alteration of school premises.

Thereafter there are few minuted references to education until the post-World War II period. It is worth noting a request in 1949 to the County Council for the provision of nursery education in the village; the reply turning the idea down was received in 1950. When the county produced a structure plan in 1960 envisaging the growth of East Leake to 4000 by 1971, one of the main concerns was that the education system could not take the strain of such a population increase and council wrote urgently to County Hall on the subject. In November 1968, an oblique reference is made to the forth-coming comprehensivisation of Harry Carlton School; council looks forward to the prospect of joint-use leisure facilities, though it is a very long term prospect, 1973 being mentioned.

At each stage in its history of enlargement the council notes approvingly the growing status of Harry Carlton School. In April 1979, a letter from Mr C J Robinson regarding imminent staff cutting at Harry Carlton provoked a searching letter to the county council demanding explanations. But it is a less happy story at the primary end of things. Council strenuously opposed the re-zoning proposals of 1976, brought about by the uneven residential growth of the village, and was not at all satisfied that nursery provision, when it came, should be at the Lantern Lane site. These last illustrate the thesis that while council could act as a mouthpiece, it could certainly not depend on being heard.

The Parish Council

If its dealings with major authorities show East Leake Parish Council ready to fight the corner of its parishioners, then there is equal evidence that it did the same with other "goliaths". For instance, there are numerous examples of letters and demands to the GPO, which resulted in the maintenance of a postal service beyond the wildest dreams of a modern letter-writer; a telegraph office which was opened at the railway station in 1902, and the provision of phone boxes at a quite generous level.

It is the way that council embraced the possibilities of the railway, which arrived just after the council itself, and the boldness with which it asserted the right of the villagers of East Leake not to be messed about, which prompt the most serious regrets about "what might have been" in the whole Parish Council story.

Council entered into correspondence about the exact desirable routing of the Normanton Hills cutting, negotiated about the siting of East Leake station, discussed the route northwards which at one time would have involved two bridges, over Gotham Road as well as Stocking Lane, and outstandingly demanded and got compensation for the blocking up of the ancient right of way from East Leake to West Leake via Fox Hills. In 1898, the Manchester, Sheffield & Lincoln Railway (as it then was, soon to be the Great Central) offered £150; Council said what about £200, and the predictable £175 paid for the surfacing of Station Road with enough left over to kerb the south side of Main Street from Gotham Road to the post office.

Two generations later the council was less successful, but just as doughty, when attempting to fight off Beeching's cuts. Rumours started in 1959, and in pre-emptive mode the Parish Council wrote to Basford and the British Transport Commission insisting that East Leake needed a half-hourly local commuter train service. It subscribed to the Great Central Users' Committee, wrote vehemently to Martin Redmayne MP and to Lord Lanesborough in support of his campaign, and protested in every appropriate forum, including a television appearance by Rev Kirton and Cllr John Langham. Indeed, in 1964 one year's reprieve for the line was announced, and this staggered on till 1968, but the next reference in the minutes is for 14th June 1972 when the dilapidated state of the disused railway station prompted a letter to British Rail asking for it to be made safe.

Rail has been displaced by road and air on the twentieth century travel scene, and here the Parish Council's attitude has been largely negative. As early as 1907 it was appealing to the County Council to designate the road from Costock to the station as a "main road", because the increased wear and tear of railway-generated traffic was creating maintenance expense it thought should not be borne solely by the parish unfortunate enough to have these lorries lumbering through. The financial burden of repairing approach roads actually fell on the district council, while the parish looked after its own streets. From then on, council has fought a losing battle against the car, trying to provide parking spaces, trying to discourage drivers from causing danger to others through speeding or general mayhem through bad parking, sorting out abandoned vehicles and so on. It suggested having a roundabout at the bottom of Castle Hill (1949) or at the junction of Woodgate Road and Kirk Ley (1958), it proposed installing "courtesy" road signs on our entry roads (Frank Godber, 1979) and times without number the County Council has been approached to look at our streets and paint more double yellow lines.

The council always seem to have viewed our proximity to East Midlands Airport as an unmitigated disaster, and has associated itself with various groups lobbying against training flights, runway extensions and the like – a protest letter in 1975, moral support for an Action Group formed in 1979, backed up by £130 in September 1980 to help in the presentation of the group's case at a public inquiry (other parish councils, eg Kegworth, it may be noted, argued their own case without relying on a citizens' pressure group).

As representatives of the village, the Parish Council might be expected to articulate responses to the great issues of the day, world events which shape the future. But, as has been mentioned, the first reference to World War I came in April 1915 in relation to the need to darken the streets. Later in 1915, there was a more positive response to Lord Derby's recruiting scheme. Canvassers were appointed and cards delivered house to house, and sadly it may be that the disproportionately heavy casualty toll among East Leake's young men owes something to this enthusiasm. At home, in January 1917, the Notts Agricultural War Committee was offering seed potatoes to "small growers". Council promoted this and put in a request for a creditable 2½ tons, made possible by a concerted effort to clear dykes. It has to be admitted, however, that the following season it refused to participate at all. In parallel, the council set up a "Sparrow & Rat Club", to safeguard "valuable food for the country in this serious time of trouble". It offered:

- eggs and unfledged birds 2d per dozen
- old sparrows 3d per dozen
- rat tails 4d per dozen

When peace came, the initiative to build some sort of memorial came from the Church Council. The Parish Council was quick to support a public meeting at which it insisted that any fund-raising would be voluntary and thereafter it was the Memorial Committee and the Town Lands Trust between them who organised the obelisk and its surrounding gardens which were opened on 23rd March 1932.

Before council had to face the trauma of World War II, there were periods of depression and unemployment to cope with. In 1924 a major land drainage scheme was proposed by the County Council, but East Leake refused to join in unless West Leake and Kingston did so too, and this in spite of a two thirds subsidy offered to riparian owners. By 1932, however, the tune had changed. Council was happy to accept seed potatoes and fertilisers from the County Council (13th December 1932) and at the same meeting, it was resolved:

"This Council view with alarm the great increase in unemployment in the village and urge that the County Council should take immediate steps either by road work or other methods to absorb unemployed labour and so relieve distress which otherwise will become acute during the winter".

The council also appealed to the Town Lands Trust to release funds for the purchase of coal and food.

World War II was, as it were, seen coming, far more than its predecessor. Council was responding to preliminary advice about air-raid shelters and gas-mask distribution from as early as March 1938. It put civil defence orders into operation, so that all road signs disappeared. It prepared for and received many evacuees (and complained to the bus company that these youngsters needed more transport). When the inevitable approach came from the Notts War Agricultural Committee, the letter was passed smartly to the Allotment Holders Association; the Parish Council was not going to be embarrassed twice.

Celebrations for the end of the war do not figure strongly in the minutes. A meeting was convened by council, but the assumption must be that any practical effort was left as before to voluntary organisations. However, the council caught the determinedly optimistic national mood of the times when it devoted just over a 2d rate to the Festival of Britain in 1951, and reckoned "a good show had been made".

East Leake's attitude to royal occasions, when flag-waving and street parties are supposed to signal popular satisfaction, can only be described as ambivalent. In 1897, council was fairly enthusiastic about Queen Victoria's Diamond Jubilee and agreed to look for a suitable commemorative playing field (unsuccessfully, as it turned out) and wrote a letter of congratulation.

A voluntary coronation committee organised some tree planting in 1902 for Edward VII, but council declined to have anything to do with it, or to help with maintenance of the trees later. In 1929, it did agree to fence a "Coronation Tree", presumably planted in 1909 in honour of George V. When it came to his Silver Jubilee in 1934, council called a parish meeting, where the decision was taken to build the village hall – opportunism of the first order, since this had been a village ambition for years, had been actively planned since 1931, and the bulk of the funds was already in the bank. In 1937 council raised 1d rate in order to celebrate George VI's coronation; the minutes do not record how it was spent, but some tree planting is referred to in November.

For his daughter Elizabeth II's coronation in 1953, the mood was decidedly up-beat; there were children's sports, a fancy dress parade, old folks' party, a concert, a dance, and a tree was planted in the Memorial Gardens – it all cost £181, and council made a profit on the 4d rate they voted for it.

There was a dance for the Silver Jubilee in 1977, and school children received gifts, but the decision to use funds from a defunct Amenities Society to repair some seats seems to lack a little as a loyal gesture. Perhaps consciences pricked, because in November council agreed to purchase for £200 the carving 'Father & Son' as a commemorative gift to the village; this statue, which is now in the library, was carved by "Ginger" Birch of Gould's Barn and his widow Ellen offered the Parish Council the chance to buy it. For the Royal Wedding in 1981, the council contented itself with flying the union flag and sending a telegram to the palace.

Probably the most enduring and visible of all Parish Councils' commitments are to do with recreation. Some allotments were started in 1896, but the Allotment Act of 1907 put things on a more formal footing. Twenty applications were received and council sought land from Mr Towson (Gotham Road), Mr Oldershaw (Castle Hill), Mr Angrave and Mr Potter, with the following result:

19th July 1909 - "Answers from the 4 gentlemen that was written to re the letting of land for allotments. Mr Potter was willing to sell to the Parish Council the three-cornered field occupied by Mr Baumber, Mr Towson stating the field asked for would spoil a small holding but if he was inclined to let it would be to the Parish Council and not to the applicants. Mr Oldershaw declined as the field in question was not his but his daughter's and Mr Angrave offered the piece of land on the north side of West Leake Road, viz 4¼ acres to the Parish Council for £700, and it was decided that nothing could be done in respect of those 4 fields. A letter was received from Mr Thompson of Loughborough offering to either let or sell the piece of land adjoining the cottages on the West Leake Road, viz 3½ acres either in large or small lots to the applicants at a very reasonable price ... viz 4d per yard".

Allotments have featured in village life ever since, with varying prosperity, and the present Allotment Holders Association is just the most recent of an honourable line.

East Leake had children's play areas before it had adult sports fields. In 1910, council received a letter from Mr Oldershaw announcing that he had bought a field at Town End which he proposed giving to the children of East Leake as a playground; the council immediately formed a recreation committee to look after it, the first task being to fence it (Cumberland & Hobbs charged £28 5s 0d). Since 1967, this playground has been the Oldershaw Trust and the Parish Council has run it as trustees.

There must have been some attempt made at organised adult sports in the earlier part of the century because when, in 1926, the Rural Community Council wrote urging East Leake to form a club for sports, games, lectures etc, they were tartly informed that several such efforts had failed in the past, and the village was not interested. Mr Neil of the Playing Fields Association was received in more friendly fashion in 1931. He spoke encouragingly of grants and cheap loans, compulsory purchase powers and money to be made. The Parish Council agreed to join the association for 5s 0d per annum and almost embarked on a comprehensive joint project with the Village Hall Committee which would have created a proper "middle" for the village with public buildings sensibly grouped and leisure facilities close by. Unfortunately, that was only the first of many missed opportunities, as the two organisations made excuses about autonomy and the difficulties of mixing charitable with local government functions. There was much ill-feeling and misunderstanding, the copious minuting of which makes unhappy reading. The saga ran for decades before the Parish Council was able in the late '70s to negotiate with the Charity Commissioners the way forward that was in all probability available all the time if anyone had been sufficiently bold to look for it.

The PT & Recreation Act of 1937 gave more powers to local authorities to provide sites for sports and to assist financially, and in the post-war period much progress was made. The first exploratory meeting towards a Playing Fields Association was in October 1948, and in November the parish council decided to apply for a 50% Ministry of Education grant towards the purchase of what became Costock Road playing fields. All parties worked at fund-raising on the one hand and the hard work of levelling, seeding and so on, on the other, and were rewarded in that in 1963 the Playing Fields Association became an official charity. In 1966 a smart new pavilion was formally opened by the parish council as its contribution to the complex. Unfortunately, they did not all live happily ever after, and only recently another playing fields charity has risen from the long-cold ashes of the earlier venture, after years of management by the parish council, during which time the playgroup and the youth club as well as the sports clubs were its tenants. In the intervening period, of course, council was involved in the establishment of other sports facilities in combination with borough or county, and the notion of a free-standing parish enterprise now seems very old-fashioned.

There has been a dramatic change in sporting opportunity and interest during the lifetime of the parish council, but one feature of recreational activity that has not changed at all is that people like to walk. The council's role in protecting our rights of way, seeing that footpaths are reasonably maintained, fixing stiles and bridges, and clearing bridle-ways has continued the same for a century, and the minutes are peppered with references to this.

This function of the parish council is not its most important, but it forms a constant theme along with, surprisingly, recurring complaints about vandalism and the lack of adequate policing. *Plus ça change ...!* The minutes reveal a succession of concerned people who were never able to achieve what parishioners expected of them. They tended to procrastinate, and they certainly suffered the procrastination of others: in March 1971, for instance, four residents presented ideas for an "imaginative playground" at Gotham Road. Council was interested, thought about it and accepted a tender for £658 in February 1972. It then took so long to build that some items had been vandalised and removed altogether by the time it underwent its first safety assessment as a so-called completed project in 1978.

Part of the problem was surely the financial straitjacket of a very limited income, which meant that the council was beholden to the senior authorities to an inhibiting extent. There would all too easily develop a downward spiral of apathy and indifference which could not possibly inspire that respect of the villagers which would in its turn stimulate greater enterprise on the part of the council. But there was a more radical structural problem, which has not been touched upon at all. This was the method by which councillors were elected. In respect of local government elections, the Representation of the People Act, 1945, obliged parishes to observe a secret ballot. Before this came into force in 1948, written nominations (themselves an innovation in 1937) had to be submitted to the annual parish meeting and after a brief question and answer session with the candidates, election was by show of hands, unless two electors demanded a poll, which was expensive and was called for only once, in 1910, when the annual meeting had gone so badly that a resolution was sent to the County Council:

"...[that a] Council so illegally elected does not meet with the approval of the main body of the ratepayers and that in the opinion of this Council (ie the outgoing Council) it would be detrimental to the best interests of the village being with one exception wholly Socialist or Radical, that the greater proportion of such Council are not direct ratepayers, the Assessed Rate Collection Act of 1869 being adopted".

The County Council declared the meeting to have been invalid, a new election was held, a poll was demanded, a rather different panel emerged (Appendix 2) and the parish got a bill for £7 6s 10d. Not only did the open system limit the electorate to those who managed to turn up on the night but, what was worse, the lack of secrecy put unfair pressure on voters whose livelihoods might well depend on voting with the bosses and it prevented potentially good candidates from offering themselves. From time to time there was a concerted effort to change, as in 1946 when the Labour Party took every place (Appendix 2), illustrating, incidentally, the importance of the railway in East Leake, with seven railwaymen or ex-railwaymen among them. To celebrate, the first minutes of that council's term were written in red ink. Their deliberations were not noticeably different from what came before or after.

APPENDIX I — CHAIRMEN AND CLERKS

Dates	Chairman	Dates	Chairman
1894 - 97	Ezra Pidcock	1939 - 41	Ernest Fletcher
1898 - 99	Morton Handley	1942 - 45	Samuel Crosland
1900	Revd Sidney Potter	1946 - 48	Edwin F G Brown
1901 - 06	Ezra Pidcock	1948 - 51	Dr H A Summers
1907	Mark W Mills	1952 - 59	Frank Godber
1908 - 09	George Goodband	1960 - 63	John Langham, DSO
1910	John Bamber	1964 - 65	J D Crosland
1911	Ezra Pidcock	1966 - 72	R N Raynor
1912	A Whitby	1972 - 77	John Langham, DSO
1913 - 19	Oswald Kirk	1977 - 83	J C Cursham
1920 - 23	Franklin Hine	1983 - 89	K L O'Toole
1924 - 30	J H North	1989 - 91	Bryan Davis
1931 - 36	H C Carlton	1991 - 95	John Needham
1937 - 38	Capt A Roulstone	1995 -	Mrs N M Jacques

East Leake Parish Council Chairmen

Dates	Clerk	Dates	Clerk
1894 - 95	Edwin Mills	1949 - 59	S Bramley
1896 - 1912	Oswald Kirk	1960	D Silcock
1913 - 1919	George R Kirk	1961 - 63	L J Kirk
1920 - 22	Fred Wass		W H Spurr
1923 - 26	Arnold Wass	1963 - 72	J C de Vine
1927 - 39	Arthur Wass	1973 - 75	C B McGregor
1940 - 48	L Harper	1975 - 77	A J Hallam
	During Mr Harper's absence	1977 - 92	L V Heath
	on active service, his wife	1992	T H Forrester-Coles
	took over his duties	1992 -	Graham T C Jones

East Leake Parish Council Clerks

APPENDIX 2 — COUNCIL MEMBERSHIP AT VARIOUS TIMES

First election		Second election ordered by County Council after complaints	
Member	Votes*	Member	Votes
Harry Hill	38	Mr Baumber	
Ezra Pidcock	38	Mr Dumelow	
George Goodband	34	Mr Chapman	
Arthur Whitby	31	Mr M Mills	
Edgar Tyers	28	Mr Handley	Votes
Frank Bramley	25	Mr Pidcock	were not
William Powdrill	25	Mr North	minuted
George Valance	25	Mr Price	
Frederick Warner	21	Mr Smith	
George Chapman	20	Mr Wass	
William Price	20	Mr Whitby	

* Note small number of parishioners present and voting

Council Membership in 1910

Member	Job	Votes	Member	Job	Votes
Edgar Scotney Tyers	Signal man	23	Frank Thomas Kirk	Farmer	14
Annie Zöe Gray*	Married woman	20	John Hallam North	Retired	13
Harry Charles Carlton	Company director	18	James Weston	Not recorded	14
Harry William Charman	Gardener	18	John Arthur Bramley	Wicker worker	12
Arthur Tebbutt Cresswell	Not recorded	15	Daniel Leivers	Schoolmaster	10
Arthur Marshall	Factory hand	15			

* First and for a long time the only female councillor   35 electors attended

Council Membership on 9th March 1931

The Parish Council

Member	Job	Votes	Member	Job	Votes
G H Crook	Butcher	92	A Marshall	Publican	72
Alexander Roulstone	Company secretary	90	F L Crowson	Dairyman	60
E Fletcher	Manager	88	F E Crosland	Lace salesman	59
E A Rayment	Grocer	85	H W Charman	Gardener	54
Gerald Wilson	Baker	83	Harry Mills	Builder	54
W Strutt	Gypsum worker	73			

The above members thought they were elected for three years, but World War II intervened. There were numerous changes due to death or resignation during the nine years that this Parish Council held office and replacements were co-opted as necessary.

Council Membership in 1937

Member	Address	Job	Votes
Edwin F C Brown	West Leake Road	*Railway worker	27
Harry W Charman	West Leake Road	Market gardener	21
Stanley James	Main Street	Joiner	19
Albert Brown	Hotchley Bungalows	*Railway worker	18
Albert Goddard	Kirk Ley Road	Agricultural contractor	18
Charles W Gubbins	Woodgate Road	*Signalman	18
Edgar Scotney Tyers	Main Street	*Retired railwayman	18
Harry Goodacre	School Green	*Railway worker	17
Stanley Albert Huss	Rempstone Road	*Railway ganger	17
Albert Edward Osborne	Kirk Ley Road	*Signalman	17
Bernard Savage	Woodgate Road	Farm worker	17

The first post-war election, still determined by show of hands.
A very small turn-out on this accasion with sixteen candiates for the eleven seats.
*Seven railway employees. One of the losing candidates was Thomas Little, station master.

Council Membership in 1946

APPENDIX 3 — EXAMPLES OF FINANCE AT VARIOUS STAGES IN THE COUNCIL'S HISTORY

20TH APRIL 1896

Caretaker, 14 nights @ 6 d (schoolroom for meetings)	7s 0d
Solicitor	£1 14s 0d
Clerk (travel expenses to auditor)	3s 0d
Clerk for postages	8s 6d
TOTAL	£2 12s 10d
Balance in hand	£4 6s 5d
Clerk to be paid	£5 per annum

30TH MARCH 1899

General account

W Wass	£6 13s 0d
Guarantee for Treasurer	6s.0d
Election fee	13s 0d
Book, stationery	13s 8d
Copy of Registrar	3d
Chairman's expenses	6s 0d
Clerk's salary	£7 1s 0d
Stamps	2s 0d
Audit stamp	10s 0d
Caretaking	3s 6d
TOTAL	£16 8s 5d

Lighting account

W Mills (oil)	£5 3s 1½d
G Moore (lamps)	£9 15s 6d
Handley (paint lamps)	13s 0d
Cousins (lamplighter)	£7 13s 0d
W Pepper (repairs, tin)	4s 0d
Rate books	10s 6d
Rate collection	£2 10s 0d
Acknowledgement for Church and Chapel lamp	6d / 6d
Magistrate's fee	2s 0d
Stamps	6d
TOTAL	£26 12s 7½d

In three years the budget had gone up by something of the order of 700%.

In 1909, the general account had gone down significantly, and the lighting account was only increase because gradually more lamps were being installed.

General account	£7 10s 6d
Lighting account	£32 18s 10d

THE PARISH COUNCIL

17TH MARCH 1931 ONWARDS

General account			Lighting account		
Income		£27 13s 9d	Income		£68 8s 1d
Expenditure		£11 8s 8d	Expenditure		£45 5s 6d
	Balance	£16 5s 1d		Balance	£23 2s 5d

The Parish Council has always made a virtue of thrift; while it was and is their duty to run the village carefully, it has at times become an inhibiting obsession.

In 1932, a 1d rate was estimated to yield £16.

In 1940, a new Clerk was appointed, at £5 per annum, rising to £15 in 1946, £22 10s 0d in 1949 and £30 in 1950. As the village expanded, so did his duties. By 1960 his fee was £52 and 1961 it rose again to £78.

Precept	for 1958	for 1960	for 1961
General	£260	£86	£280 (2d rate)
Lighting	£608	£605	£350 (2½d rate)

1967 — the increased size of the village meant that a 1d rate now yielded £705, but expenditure was also increased; a 4d rate was needed in 1969 (£2720).

In 1975, precept was for a 1p (now decimal currency) rate (£5120).

In 1976 precept, again 1p, based on the following:

Estimated balance 31/3/76	£2684.87
Estimated income 1976/77	£7340.26
Estimated expenditure 1976/77	£4845.65
Estimated net income	£2494.61
Estimated balance 31/3/77	£5179.48

1995/96 council tax precept calculated by fixed formula, yield approximately £53000.

BIBLIOGRAPHY

Rev Sidney Pell Potter (1903), *A History of East Leake*, W B Cooke, Nottingham

Dr Robert Thoroton, 1623 - 78 (1677), *The Antiquities of Nottinghamshire, extracted out of records, original evidence, leiger books, other manuscripts and authentic authorities*, H Mortlock, London

Dr Robert Thoroton, 1623 - 1678 (1790), *The Antiquities of Nottinghamshire*, Three volumes, edited and enlarged by John Thorsby, 2nd edition (1972) with a new introduction by M W Barley and K S S Train, E P Publishing Ltd (for Nottinghamshire County Library), Wakefield

Malcolm Todd (1973), *The Coritani*, Gerald Duckworth & Co Ltd, London

Chris Weir (1991), *The Nottinghamshire Heritage*, Phillimore & Co Ltd, Chichester

A C Wood (1947), *A History of Nottinghamshire*, S R Publishers, Nottingham

Domesday Book (1977), 28, *Nottinghamshire*, Phillimore and Co Ltd, Chichester

Graham Black and David Rolfe (1986), *The Nottinghamshire Domesday — A Reader's Guide*, City of Nottingham Arts Department, Nottingham

Lord Ernle (1922), *English Farming Past and Present*, Longman Green & Co, London

G M Trevelyan (1944), *English Social History*, Longman Green & Co, London

Warwick Rodwell (1989), *Church Archeology*, R T Batsford & Co Ltd, London

R Owen Wood (1993), *St Mary's Church, East Leake — Its History*, Parochial Church Council, East Leake

Nottinghamshire Family History Society (1981), Vol XIII, *Monumental Inscriptions*, Technical Print Services Ltd, Nottingham

Publications of East Leake and District Local History Group:

    R Owen Wood, *The Roads, Trackways and Footpaths of East Leake*, 1999

    The Leake Historian, Volumes 1 to 4, 1993 - 1998

    East Leake Families — Some 19th Century Farmers, 1995

The primary records, ie census returns, registers of birth, marriages and deaths, and other records relating of East Leake are held at the local library and by the local history group. Archive material such as wills, inventories and public records are scattered between the county archives of Derbyshire, Leicestershire and Nottinghamshire.

PERSONAL NOTES

Personal Notes

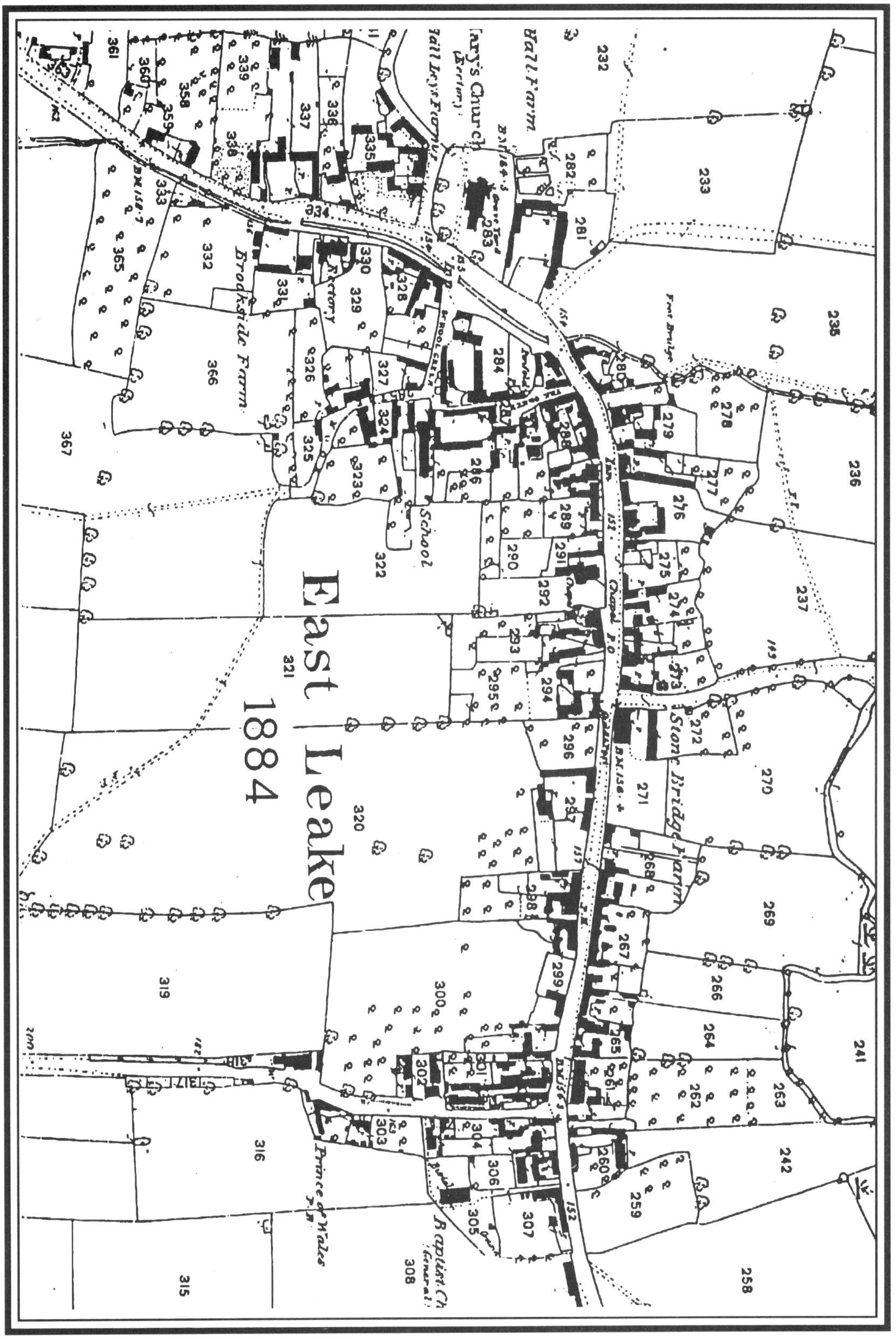
East Leake
1884
School
Rectory
Brookside Farm
Hall Farm
Stone Bridge Farm
Prince of Wales
Baptist Ch
Foot Bridge

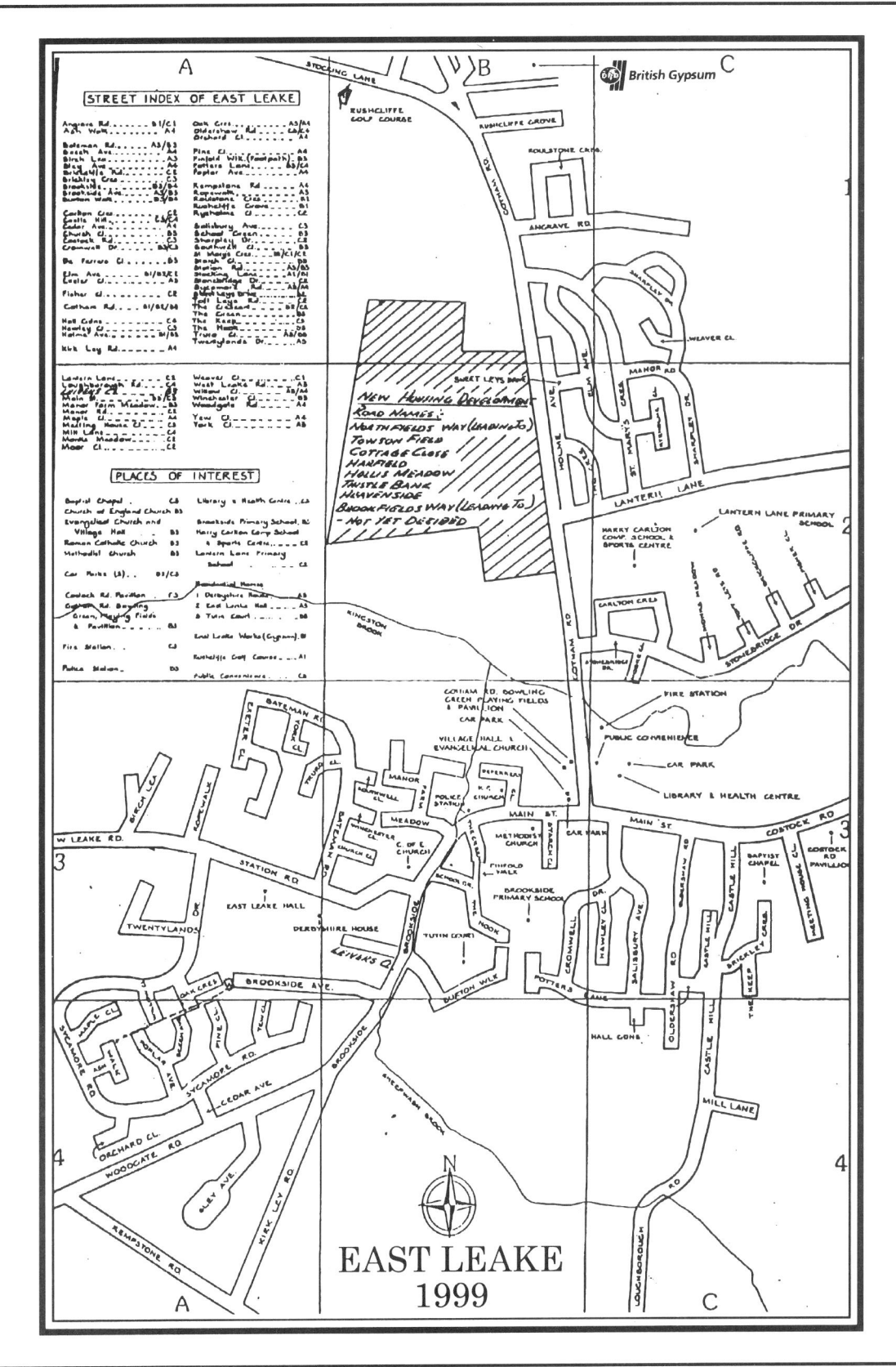

EAST LEAKE 1999